THE STORY
OF
QUEEN GUINEVERE
AND
SIR LANCELOT OF THE LAKE.

AFTER THE GERMAN OF WILHELM HERTZ.

WITH OTHER POEMS.

BY CHARLES BRUCE.

LONDON:
LONGMAN, GREEN, LONGMAN, ROBERTS, & GREEN.
1865.

In the interest of creating a more extensive selection of rare historical book reprints, we have chosen to reproduce this title even though it may possibly have occasional imperfections such as missing and blurred pages, missing text, poor pictures, markings, dark backgrounds and other reproduction issues beyond our control. Because this work is culturally important, we have made it available as a part of our commitment to protecting, preserving and promoting the world's literature. Thank you for your understanding.

PREFACE.

THIS little volume is put into your hands, Beautiful Being! that you may be amused.

It was intended to contain only the Story of Queen Guinevere and Sir Lancelot. I have, however, determined to add to this some other poems—an earnest, I trust, of better things.

Let me call them splinters from the lever of Love, with which I hope some time to move the World—if I had a place to stand on!

Standing over the grave of buried affections and lost hopes, surely I shall not wholly fail.

CHARLES BRUCE.

13 BRUTON STREET: *April* 8, 1865.

CONTENTS.

	PAGE
QUEEN GUINEVERE AND SIR LANCELOT OF THE LAKE	1
ROLAND AND BLANCHEFLEUR	167
ADONIS	190
PET NAMES	199
LOLA	203
EFFIE	208
THE EYES WHICH JESUS LOVED	218
GOOD NIGHT	226

X

Where are the cheeks, white as wool, red as scarlet
    In blanching and blushing?
Where are the cheeks that I touched, purely starlit,
    And felt their red flushing?
Where are the cheeks that flushed red for me,
    Red for me?

Where are the eyes on whose closed lids, love-laden,
    The blue veins beat, in hurried
Vibration, as fondly my lips kissed the maiden
    From cheek, chin, and forehead?
Where is the light dear eyes shed for me,
    Shed for me?

Where are the tresses whose fragrance still lingers,
    By a power unseen holden?
Where are the hands, and the soft rosy fingers,
    Behind my head folden?
Where art thou, O Love? whither fled for me,
    Fled for me?

Slow are the swift feet that sped for me,
    Sped for me:
Bitter the things sweet lips said for me,
    Said for me!

Cold are the cheeks that flushed red for me,
    Red for me:
Gone is the light dear eyes shed for me,
    Shed for me!

Soft hands, rosy fingers are fled for me,
    Fled for me:
And thou, Love, for ever art dead for me,
    Dead for me!

May 6, 1865.

QUEEN GUINEVERE AND SIR LANCELOT OF THE LAKE.

I.

PEACE rests upon King Arthur's land,
For every foe is over-manned,
And every fiend and monster crushed,
The flight of wild adventures hushed.
The sultry hours of trial passed,
Has Perceval the Graal at last;
Long since in haunted Brocelind
Left Merlin name and fame behind;
Sir Ivain seeks, his madness fled,
The lady of the fountain's bed;
And Erec leads a listless life
Of dalliance by his gentle wife;

And Arthur gladly whiles away,
With games and pageant pomps, the day.
At Camalot, where the vale is green,
His summer hall of knights is seen:
There, round the aged monarch flies
The light of gentle star-bright eyes;
There rise, like knotted forest oak,
His battle-statured warrior folk.
Yet, save the warfare that love wages,
Fight now no more their thought engages;
For in the hero's thought
Love holds its camp and court,
And men, whose arms could death-blows deal
On giants, woman's chains must feel.

For in the storm of battle tossed,
Man's heart ne'er yet its freedom lost;
But peaceful charms have oft undone
The conquest strength hath dearly won;
When peace asserts its sacred ban,
Then woman lords it over man.

SIR LANCELOT.

Thus glode the happy years away
In dalliance and in sportive play,
And spring with its serenest blue
Was bursting o'er the land anew;
When many a hero's limbs were fain
To don their ancient arms again,
And, heavy still with sleep, essay
Their puissance in the knightly fray.
Then many a guest did Arthur call
To tournament and festival,
And at his summons thousands hied
To Camalot at Whitsuntide.

'Twas in the golden month of May,
Loud rose the murmur of tournay,
And sword, and shield, and splintering spear,
Rang music on the eager ear.
Full many a war-horse there went down,
And many a knight was overthrown,
And dragged away, with whom, I crede,
These jovial May-games scarce agreed.

But one was there, whose spear before,
No saddle long its burden bore;
His helmèd head towered over all,
Ne'er stained by an inglorious fall:
His shield, in gold on azure, bore,
' Haut de naissance, de vaillance et d'Amour ; '
His light blue harness flashed afar,
As swift he thrid the tangled war;
His steed tramped way where'er it trod,
And splinters rattled as he rode.
One saw both dame and maiden cast
Their sweetest glances as he past,
And many a heedless mouth exprest
The gentle wishes of the breast;
Now praised his valiant arm in fight,
The comely stature of the knight,
His kingly bearing, gracious nod,
As grandly through the lists he rode,
And, when his thigh the saddle pressed,
His war-horse snorted in unrest.

But nought he heeded what they said—
The light of his proud eye was staid,
Among that fair array, on one
Who sat on Arthur's splendid throne :
The red gold round her golden hair
Proclaimed her Queen and Empress there !
No maiden she, with shame opprest,
Whose eye falls coyly on her breast :
A stately dame, in life's full phase,
Bright-burning like the noon-day blaze.
'T would seem that garment scarce might hold
A form of such imperial mould,
Which, conscious of its victories won,
Seemed labouring like the silent sun—
Proud, inapproachable—to show
Its glories to a world below.
Where lay the land that knew not her—
The far-famed, glorious Guinevere?
'T was she—the Queen of Camalot !
Men called her knight, Sir Lancelot.

A weary old man she had wed—
A green graft on a tree long dead.
Her gentle heart was reconciled
To love him, as she were his child;
But all that fans love bridal fires,
And swells the waves of youth's desires,—
That weds the manly to the fair,—
Makes youth with youth a comely pair,—
Long since in Arthur died away:
His heart was cold, his head was gray;
But she was in life's glowing spring,
And long'd for love, a passioned thing;
All love's sweet fancies teemed in her,
And Lancelot was young and fair.

How proudly beats her heart—how free—
On this new day of victory!
The people scream—the heralds shout—
While pealing trumpets thunder out,
'The joust is out—the prize is his!'
Her heart exultant echoes—his!

Sir Lancelot swings him from his horse,
Through crowding pages wends his course
To the pavilion where she stands,
The victor's garland in her hands;
While sunset's glories, ere they die,
Shine purple in her lovelit eye.
A wreath of roses, fresh and red,
She twines around his helmèd head;
Holds out to him a blue surcoat,
With broidery her own hands have wrought;
And gives—the rule of tournay this—
Her queenly brow for him to kiss.
The flush that glows upon his cheek,
Of bashful pleasure seems to speak.
How many a livelong summer-day
Had Lancelot whiled the hours away,
His guilty lips on hers imprest,
And rocked on her enamoured breast!
But now he well might dare to bow,
And kiss that loved imperial brow,

This riddle rede me if ye can—
He pauses like a guilty man;
And, as that tender mouth he feels,
His shuddering heart in unrest reels;
For just as when love's lightning, shot
From some dark eye, a heart hath smote,
His soul inebriate seems with bliss,
As this had been their earliest kiss.

Exchanging tokens of salute,
With smiling countenance and mute,
They stand as if on charmèd ground,
In longing, lingering gaze spell-bound;
While round their fair young foreheads plays
The red gold of the sun's last rays.

Far off, in his pavilion,
Leant Mordred, Arthur's sister's son.
In arms that warrior had grown old—
A mighty form of giant mould;
His hair fell raven-black and thick,
Around his dark and bearded cheek;

'Neath bushy brows his eyeballs rolled,
His close drawn mouth defiance told.
Bent o'er his sword, in angry mood,
Amid the crowd of knights he stood;
The tokens of his features tell
That he hath never loved too well.
Ascetic, uncomplaining, lone
He lives—all joy to him unknown;
A knightly deed in knightly hour—
The exultant pomp of youthful power—
He deems but idle pride, that lies
Concealed beneath Hell's gay disguise.
The power of Faith that he can feel
Is Strength, he knows, not worlds shall steal.
He early left the court's gay rout,
And wandered in strange lands about,
A wild life with some Viking host
He led, on stormy waters tost;
And just returned, he marks, with pain,
How warriors serve and women reign.

But anger burnt his soul within,
To watch the conduct of the Queen:
His spying eyes glowed hot, to scan
The falsehood of the wife and man—
How openly they dare rehearse,
Unshamed, their guilt and Arthur's curse,
And fan the spark of their desire
With meaning tokens into fire;
With sin they scarcely care disguise,
The laws of God and man despise.

'Alas! my uncle, there is not
A soul from Rome to Camalot,
But tells by land and sea the name
Which meaneth Guinevere's great shame.
To Arthur, and to him alone—
The hoary, blind old man—unknown,
This day the tidings he shall hear;
And breathe out curses on the year
When first he planned to make his court
A place for such unhallowed sport;

Forgetful, in these dalliant hours,
Of manhood's rights and manhood's powers.
Methinks, *that* time may now be past,
And love of arms take heart at last,
And rather than that love pass by,
May all the house of Arthur die!'

   The drums are beat, the trumpet blows,
The bright procession gaily goes—
Queen Guinevere mounts horse, and deigns
To let Sir Lancelot hold the reins.

II.

That night, King Arthur's castle hall
Was gay with dance and festival:
Each chamber, hall, and corridor,
Bright flaming torch and taper bore,
And, where the river glode along,
Was laughter heard and mirth and song.
On many a swift and gay canoe
The pendulous lamps their brightness threw,
While merry pages joyed to lave
Their snow-white limbs in that cool wave.
Meanwhile were held, in mimic sport,
The moonlight sessions of Love's Court;
And whispering lovers wandered through
The dark and bowery avenue.
In the burgh, too, with cup and can,
Caroused the master and his man;

And gaily in the crowded inn,
They tripped it to the violin;
Where many a bold, love-prompted word
Not too unwilling maidens heard.
All nature felt the magic hour
Of spring, and that enchanting power,
Which weddeth bloom to bloom, and twines
The clasping tendrils of the vines,
And fills all things that live and move
With thoughts of longing and of love.

Two men, far off from all the rest,
Their way through pines and forests pressed.
One forward strode with angry air,
A mighty man—with raven hair;
That other—'neath gray locks was seen
An earnest-mild, imperial mien.
Close to the margin of the wood,
Just off the path a linden stood;
Here paused that swarthy man: nought wakes
Save winds that play among the brakes,

And half-lost echoes from the feast,
That murmured sadly ere they ceased.
The old man asked, in smiling mood,
' What will'st thou, Mordred, in this wood?
To blameless Arthur will'st impart
The necromancer's naughty art?
I fear we interrupt above
Some owlet's episode of love.'

That other said, ' I well nigh fear
That sweeter, both to heart and ear,
Might prove the owlet's melody
Than shall the news I have for thee.'

On him the old man laid his hold,
And dark his eye and angry rolled;
Yet Mordred flinched not from his ease,
But whispered low such words as these:
' Unholy deeds are done that bring
Disgrace on your fair fame, Sir King!
Sir Lancelot and your proud dame
Have made a jest of Arthur's name.'

The monarch cried, 'And, dar'st thou, knave,
With words like these my presence brave?
With thy false tongue suspicion rouse,
And fill with war and death my house?'

'I was prepared for this tempèst—
Truth comes not oft a bidden guest.
If I some fawner's plot had laid,
Among the revellers I had staid.
I know my words must pierce your heart;
I honour—for I feel—the smart.
I know you loved him, and believed,
Who hath so shamefully deceived.
I know you twined your love round one,
Who all that hate could do hath done.
You saw *me* with unfriendly eye—
No falsely fawning courtier I—
Now, soon enough, sire, you shall know
Who was your worst and deadliest foe;
And who—redeemed from flattery's art—
Hath loved you with a friend's warm heart.'

The old man dropped his trembling hand.
'Your proofs, Sir Nephew, I demand.'
'I ask but time, and wait your leave:
To-morrow night you *must* believe.
A hunting-morn at once proclaim,
And leave Sir Lancelot with your dame;
And tell them that the hunt will last
Until at least two days have passed.
Sir Uncle, forfeit be my head,
If further proof you then shall need;—
Then withering love shall lose its bloom,
And justice shall the sword assume.'

But meanwhile, through the Hall of Kings,
The goblets clash—the music rings;
On the soft cushions of the throne
Guinevra rests her head, alone;
Still glowing from the swift wild dance,
Her cheeks like dewy roses glance;
Over her purple robe is rolled
Her loose long hair in waves of gold;

And still more proud—more glorious seems
The fashion of her panting limbs.
Low bows Sir Lancelot to greet
The lovely dame, and at her feet
He sitteth, while she bends more near
His upturned face her willing ear.

'O let me gaze and gaze anew,
Fair lady, on thine eyes' warm blue;
That in the heaven of thy sweet face
My adoring heart may hope for grace.
Too long my cruel destiny
Hath kept its painful hand on me!
Tho', mid thy dames, each day, 'tis true,
Thy queenly beauty I may view,
I am not one that well can brook
To stand aside and calmly look.
All, all the sun-light I *can* know
From thy sweet countenance must flow;
Still, still that voice of thine I hear
Chaunt song of bridal in my ear;

And still thy bosom's rise and fall
Those consecrated nights recall,
Yet I must wait in patient sorrow
And hope—and hope, perhaps, to-morrow.'
 Soft smiles upon her fair face came,
As o'er him bent the lovely dame.
 ' You wild impetuous lover, cease
To break upon my moment's peace !
Oh ! breathe not that bold breath of thine
So warmly on these cheeks of mine !
Deem not the pain long severance brings
Thy heart and soul, thine only wrings :
Those curst, dear horrors I too feel,
While slow the sultry long nights steal.
Oh ! to be whole, with nought to sever
Me from thy healing side for ever !
Oh ! that this crown's dull joyless weight
Upon my brows no longer sate.
Suspicion in each corner lies,
The house is full of evil eyes;

At every step some spy I fear.
Yet listen: on my bosom here
This white rose and this red I bear.
This white rose shall these words announce—
"Learn, O Sir Lancelot, to renounce!"
The token of this crimson flower—
"To-morrow at the usual hour."'

That moment Arthur entered there,
And gazed not lovingly on her;
His dark eyes lightened as he spied
Sir Lancelot sitting at her side.

With angry step the monarch trod
The hall, and raised his voice aloud:—
'To-morrow, at the early dawn,
We hold, Sir Knights, a hunting-morn.
But now they brought the tidings round,
In Tarnwathlan a boar was found,
Who in our acres makes more free
Than seemeth such wild guests as he;

We'll make our claims of lordship good,
And try to spoil his merry mood!
But, ladies, as your cavalier,
We leave with you Sir Lancelot here;
And he will see what he can do
To find some pastime meet for you.
Two days, methinks, will last our sport,
And then we shall return to court.'

Low bowed Sir Lancelot, and a flame
Of pleasure lightened thro' his frame;
But not a token might one trace
Of what he felt upon his face;
For joy's wild thrill and sorrow's smart
He buried deep down in his heart.

That moment with a cup of wine
Approached the stately, brave Gawain:
'Drink, Lancelot—you are still to-night—
Methinks your duties will sit light;
But come and hearken while you can,—
I've somewhat for your ear, poor man.'

He led Sir Lancelot from the room,
And whispered words that boded doom :
' Oh, friend, be careful what you do—
The boar they mean to hunt is you !
I marked how dark the king's eye shone—
He was with Mordred long alone.
Be watchful—both in word and deed—
That parson-knight I would not crede.'

His words were scarcely done, when wide
The mighty doors were flung aside ;
By torch and taper grandly came
The monarch and his fair young dame.
In passing stately through the hall,
Guinevra let a red rose fall.

III.

'And if, this night, the powers of hell
Before thy door stood sentinel,
I'd burst hell's grimmest horrors through,
The heaven of thy sweet face to view.
Were poison in thy red lips' breath,
Must thy sweet body prove my death,
Then death should come and find me wooing
The curst, dear cause of my undoing!'

The warrior rose, and grasping tight
His naked sword, in garb of night
The empty halls he noiseless treads,
And cold dark corridors he threads,
Where its blue sheen the moonlight pours
Through vaulted arches on the floors.
No sound was heard, save now and then
The wolf's far shriek from tarn and glen,

Or from some ruined tower the howl,
Half human, of the screeching owl.
Close to the wall Sir Lancelot glode,
With cautious stretched-out hand he strode,
Till one small ray of taper fell
From threshold that he knew too well.

  Exotic flowers in that chambère
Shed spicy fragrance through the air,
And conch and shell poured mellowed light,
Not too oppressive to the sight.
Blue silken tapestry hung round
The bronzen couch-stead to the ground,
Where, dreaming the sweet hours away,
The pearl of all fair women lay.
Sunk deep in waves of golden hair,
Her head lies love-inebriate there:
Her fair white form is scarcely hid
Beneath the rosy coverlid.
She starts—sweet panic! on her brow
She felt love's gentle token glow.

Then round that wondrous blooming form,
He weaves his arms in force of storm.

Oh, night of love! how silently
Thou passest through the stars on high;
Thou sett'st a barrier to the day;
Mak'st thought in feeling die away;
With one brief hour thou can'st atone
For all that joyless fate hath done.
Oh, night of love! Thou guardian power
Of Being's first mysterious hour!
The seed thou feedest in its tomb,
And at thy touch the roses bloom,
Thy veiling shadows hide the flush
Of beauty's chaste and fearful blush.

Sweet Guinevere, in dream's dear charms,
Around him glues her clasping arms;
The thanks of love glow in the glance
Of that ecstatic countenance;
Until love's boldness is opprest
By sleep, and care disturbs her breast.

'Oh! whence these horrors when I gaze,
Sweet lover, on thy darling face?
And must my heart be still a slave,
Nor claim the rights that nature gave?
Alas! so close hell's border lies
Upon my land of Paradise,
That I, to steal one kiss away,
The awful price of sin must pay.'

  The warrior stroked his darling's head,
And fondly gazing, thought and said:
'I mark that in thy heart this hour
Gives tokens of its angry power;
The king hath hearkened treachery hiss,
And we must bid farewell to peace.
But if I leave you now—oh! when,
My darling, shall we meet again?
For spying eyes will lurk about,
Within the palace and without;
And hate and jealousy will draw
Against our love the sword of war.

But now it must be so, I fear,
We two must part, sweet Guinevere!
The demon Discord, hovering o'er
Our heads, shall haunt this house no more;
For I will wander far and wide,
And hope in patience good may tide.
I feel, I know that nought can sever
My life from thine, sweet love, for ever.
For thou art mine—this creed I feel,
Not king nor priest can ever steal;
In this wide world no bond can prove
So holy as the bond of love.'

  He bends him o'er her dreamily,
And drinks the bright tear from her eye—
Hark! thundering thro' the silent night,
The door resounds with blows of might;
And steps are heard along the hall,
And clash of arms and hoarser bawl.
Half-dead for fright, the queen lies
Beneath the couch's coverlid;

But Lancelot grasps—to fury fanned—
His sword-hilt in his mighty hand.
In awful wrath the warrior rises,
For Mordred's voice he recognises:
'Sir Lancelot, we have you fast—
Who sows in folly, reaps at last.'
Swift from the door he moved the pin—
One plucky knave came storming in;
Then Lancelot forced back the door,
And drew a mighty bolt before;
Then, maddening in his rage, he ran
Toward the wholly harnessed man,
And put such strength upon the blow
As laid him in an instant low;
Stripped off his harness as he lay,
And drew it on without delay.
Her hiding-place Guinevra leaves,
And buckles on his mail and greaves.
'Man never,' cried the knight, 'I crede,
Drew on his harness with more speed!'

Then wide the jarring door he flung,
And stormed out wild his foes among;
His broadsword, as he wildly lashed,
On dirk and dagger brightly flashed.
Eleven men a barrier rear,
With lofty helm and sturdy spear;
But Lancelot seemed with joy to wield
Before his ample breast his shield.
He recked not now of lady's love,
But of the strokes with which he clove
In twain the dragon's scaly head
In days of old,—alas! long fled,—
And through the vaulted arches rang
The broadsword's merciless clear clang.
From splintering helms there redly rushed
Full fountains of hot blood that gushed,
And down the marble staircase ran,
As swiftly man fell after man;
Till Mordred's foot began to yield
As over corpse on corpse he reeled.

But still above the winding stair,
With giant strength he held him there;
Until that day he ne'er had fled,
And, pressed against the balustrade,
He strove, with grim defence and bold,
His honour and his place to hold.
He held his shield before his breast,
And forward, madly struggling, pressed;
But Lancelot, with foaming mouth,
Dealt on his neck a blow so couth,
That from his helmet round about,
The veins their fountains spirted out.
Then truly stood his heart in need—
He saw his followers dead or bleed;
Then, dark and giddy, reeled his head,
And blood-bestreamed, he turned and fled.

But meanwhile, at the din and bawl,
All woke within the castle-wall:
The women scream—men swear and shout—
The watchman's trumpet thunders out.

In anxious haste, her maidens came
To look for their imperial dame:
Who, praying, trembling, kneeling low,
Heard angry blow resound on blow.
They knelt in silence by her side,
Eager her stiffened limbs to hide;
And smoothed, not daring they to speak,
The tresses from her blanchèd cheek.

The sheen of blood his harness bore,
As Lancelot strode through the door;
Then in her heart new pulses beat —
She leapt her Lancelot to meet:

'Thou livest! then I can support
This parting's painful, blissful thought!
Now weave thy clasping arms around me—
The whole world's gaze shall not confound me!
Now all is finished: I have run
My course, and hope and fear are done;
All that restraint, which held me fettered,
Like some oppressive dream, is scattered.

Farewell! farewell! for thou must flee—
All my love's blessing goes with thee.
May dreams of happier times appear
Through the lone world thy soul to cheer!
Once more I kiss and cling to thee,
And now for ever leave I thee.'

In depth of grief, in strength of love,
Around her his great arms he wove:
'Come with me, choose the only path
From shame and chains and Arthur's wrath.'
She freed her gently from his hand:
'To-morrow waits for God's command;
But here I stay, and I will prove
The courage of heroic love.
My love he won not, could not claim,—
My soul to fear he shall not tame;
My fate, my fortune chains me here:
I will not flee—I will not fear!'

Then mute he fixed his lingering view
On that dear eye which pierced him through,

And left the room in burning haste,
While after him she fondly gazed.

But scarce he vanished from her view,
When all her heart's wound bled anew;
And by the slain that lay around,
Speechless she sank upon the ground.

A horn blows shrill—upon her head,
She feels a hand of iron laid;
Red lowers on her the fiery glance
Of Arthur's awful countenance.
He, holding Mordred with one hand,
Then with the other waved command:
'Away this woman! hide in night
Her sinful body from the light.
Before her doom brief hours shall roll—
May God have mercy on her soul.'

IV.

Red lour'd the lamplight on the wall,
In Arthur's awful judgment hall;
Thro' windows barred the pallid gray
Of dawning morn scarce stole its way;
And ghastly pale, and motionless,
The judges sat, in sable dress.
About the marble table rolled
The velvet's black and heavy fold;
And on it dagger, string, and sword,
Lay, turned the prisoner toward.
But, like a rose, whose cheerful bloom
Beams from some cavern's awful gloom,
So shone, amid that vault's dark night,
Fair Guinevere—so fair, so bright.
Her eye was raised to heaven, her thought
The judge's questions heeded not,

Until he rose in wrath and cried;
Then low, yet firmly, she replied:
'What more can my confession tell?
What has been done ye know full well.
I broke the book-laws that ye plan
So wisely for the guild of man:
Give sentence, therefore, as they teach;
And if my life must heal the breach,
Then let it end.   No sympathy
I ask; but say not this of me—
That I profaned, to my disgrace,
The heart's most consecrated place,
Unveiling to your spying eyes
My inmost being's close disguise.
If but one word, and I were free,
That word should ne'er be spoke by me.
Those books of yours cannot divine
The meaning of a love like mine.'

  An angry murmur ran among
The judges. Up the monarch sprung:

'Ye hear how this defiant thing
Would mock us with her shameful sin.
Our pardoning mercy she disdains,—
Your sentence, sirs, is all remains!'

A flush upon Guinevra's cheek
Came lightly as he ceased to speak.
The girdle bound about her waist,
The fashion of her stature traced;
Her breast, by pinioned arms exposed,
The fullness of its form disclosed;
So, calm she stood there and serene,
Like idol of some heavenly queen,
Whose marble form, in lust of war,
Barbarians raise the axe to mar.

A menial bore the ballot-urn
To those dread judges, dark and stern;
Guinevra—pearl of women—may
The God of Beauty be thy stay!

In Hellas, so the tale is told,
A lovely woman dwelt of old:

Since Helen, none so fair was seen
Beneath Ionia's heaven serene.
Ye know her—for the Muses loved,
And old Praxiteles approved,
Around her bosom's form divine
The rapture of his arms to twine.
For wonder every murmur ceased,
As once, at great Poseidon's feast,
Like new-born Aphrodite she
Rose glorious from the sacred sea.
Then after, she before the throne
Of justice stood, accused, alone :
Hyperides all vainly there
His pleading language poured for her,
And on the judges' lips there stood
The verdict that demanded blood ;—
Then from her shoulders, so they say,
That pleader touched the robe away,
Till round her girdle amply rolled
The purple's deep and massy fold ;

And so she stood, as on that day
When at her feet all Hellas lay.
Beneath the waist it just displays
The falling garment haply stays;
And through its folds more glorious seems
The fashion of her veilèd limbs.
A moment mute the speaker stands,
Then raised, inspired, his pleading hands:
'Athenians, pause before ye dare
To mar what gods have made so fair!'
In ecstasy they sat amazed,
Those judges, as on her they gazed;
And o'er them came a sacred fear—
They felt a godhead's presence near.
One only spake: 'Forgive, forgive—
And let the beauteous sinner live!
The heavenly daughter of the sea,
Who bid her do her embassy,
Hath given her beauty's spear and shield,
Before whose conquering power we yield.'

That was in Hellas—ah! what bore
That vision hence from Thespia's shore?
Like doom hangs o'er Guinevra's head,
But all those judges long are dead;
And no Olympian land hath borne
These judges by King Arthur sworn.

Not one before that wondrous form,
Feels his cold heart to mercy warm;
Not one—the hand of each lets fall
Within the urn the dread black ball.
Guinevra's lips a moment quiver.
Pale sits King Arthur, and a shiver
Smites his strong heart, those words to hear,
Which doom what once he held so dear,
What could his aged heart inspire;
For this the verdict—'Death by fire!'

A stormy morn rose pale and gray,
With fogs that on the meadows lay;
Around the church-tower throngs the crowd,
Whose eager whispers murmur loud;

While sullen sounds the Sinner's Bell
O'er peaceful fields its awful knell.
Gawain stood on a tower, apart
From all, and heavy was his heart.
He thinks what agony of shame
Has come upon the lovely dame;
He thinks of him, his friend in arms,
His friend in peace, in war's alarms;
He deems that he himself has been
Not wholly sinless in this sin.
For he had been the first to mark
In their unconscious breasts the spark
Of love, which he himself had fanned,
And for them many a meeting planned;
For it had been his pride to share
In rendering happy such a pair.
And now—ah! how was this to end?
A fugitive, proscribed, his friend;
While yonder, in the distant brake,
They pile the fagggots round the stake.

With sad, sad heart—with eyes all dim,
As there he stands, there come to him
His brothers: rosier boys are not
Among all those in Camalot.
They clasp his knees, his hands they take,
For they have a request to make.
One climbs and whispers—half in fear—
With tender kisses, in his ear:
'Dear brother, may we go with thee,
Our mistress once again to see?'

A heavy tear ran down his cheek,
Ere Gawain dared again to speak;
He kissed the boys about his knees,
Then whispered soft such words as these;

'Ah! think you your young hearts can dare
So terrible a sight to bear?
For nought but sunshine ever yet,
Those clear, pure eyes of yours have met.
Ye know not what it is to trace
The tokens of a dying face.

Ah! no, dear children, keep away,
For Queen Guinevra's rest to pray.'

Then spake the eldest, weeping sore:
'For us the day shall dawn no more
In gladness, if thus cruelly
Our gentle lady is to die.
Ah! do not then deny our prayer,
That we once more may honour her.
We only ask that we may stand,
Beside the path on either hand;
Her kindly smile once more may meet,
Once more strew flowers at her feet.
When that is done, we will away,
And pray for her by night and day.'

They kiss him—they entreat him so—
'Dear brother Gawain, let us go!'—
That he is forced to give consent.
'My servants with you shall be sent,
For I will, in my lonely room,
This hour's great anguish overcome.'

But meanwhile, through a stormy shower,
The bell rings sadly from the tower.
The king sits in his hall alone—
She goes to death—his bride—his own.
The verdict has been spoken—
The black rod has been broken.

Ah! who shall tell the vast unrest
Against the king's great heart that prest?
How stormy in his bosom strove
The waves of anger, hate, and love?
He thought of days of yore,
Of splendours now no more;
And from each picture fancy raised
That glorious face in beauty gazed,
Which made his life's late winter-day
To blossom with the rose of May.
And pity now not wholly sleeps,
And mercy trembles on his lips.
But stay!—shall Arthur be afraid
To execute the laws he made?

He knew the judges' books declare
The penalty of death for her :
And it were mockery now to fear,
That dreadful doom were too severe.
Why call the judges if he meant
To make a farce of punishment?
Shall Arthur's wife escape alone,
While others must their guilt atone?
Ah, no! let sin its guerdon gain—
The crime was great, be great the pain.
And yet, upon his head alone
Descended all that she had done :
If, therefore, Arthur shall forgive,
And let the offending sinner live,
Then joy should answer mercy's call,
Her life its blessings bring to all.
' To all—to *me* its blessings ? ` No :
For me far other fruits shall grow !
Like thief and robber shall I bear
To lurk on landing-place and stair ?

Spy out my shame in bloody sweat,
And be deceived more grossly yet!
Yes, while repentance dews her eye,
For my fair rival she will sigh;
Yes, she will clasp him—and caress,
And fondly to her bosom press—
In mockery of my hoary hair,
Will smooth his tresses—brown and fair;
And glue around him—No, descend,
Dark Night of Death, and all shall end.'

The old man pressed his mantle tight
Before his face, and through the night
Of darkness heard the pealing bell
A soothing tale of vengeance tell.

But meantime through the city gate
The dark procession moved in state,
And weeping voices in that hour
Gave token of its dreadful power.
Then through the people's close array
The spearmen scarcely forced a way,

Till in white garb of penance came
The queenly form of Arthur's dame :
Shame cast an angry, burning glance
On her deep-earnest countenance.
With naked feet she moved along,
All silent through the crowding throng,
And not a lineament gave trace
Of suffering on that queenly face,
Though tight the hangman's hand had wound
Round her white arm the cords that bound.
Two priests before her heedless eye
The Cross of Jesus held on high,
And swung their censers 'mid the throng,
And muttered sacred psalm and song.

A cry of anguish smote her ear,
And from her dream woke Guinevere.
She saw four gentle boys approach
In tears, her garment's hem to touch.
They kiss it fondly, clasp her hand,
And scatter flowers on the sand;

Cling closely to her heart, and raise
Dear, trembling eyes to meet her gaze.
She puts them from her—in her eye
A tear stands as she passes by,
While helpless in that surging throng
Of people they are borne along.

And now the sad procession's file
Draws nearer to the fearful pile;
They see the judges' caitiffs stand,
A burning torch in every hand.
Then from his side the hangman frees
His rope, his hands prepare to seize
And cut his victim's gown away,
With eye like tiger's fixed on prey.
Then from the forest thunders out
A sudden, merciless loud shout;
With lightning speed there comes across
The waste, a dark-mailed band of horse.
Before them rode a man whose mould
And giant stature plainly told

That it was he—the grandest knight
That ever carried sword in fight.
'Strike home! or Guinevere is lost!'
Upon his snorting steed he crossed,
With bloody spur, hedge, ditch, and brake—
That is Sir Lancelot of the Lake.

And as on Norway's wild hill-side,
From icy forests burst the tide
Of Berserks, maddening in their rage,
With naked arms their fight to wage—
So Lancelot blindly hurled abroad
The lightning of his flaming sword;
And fiercely, Guinevere to save,
His way amid the ranks he clave.
A gory track he left and red
Upon the grass bestrewn with dead.
He marked not where his broadsword fell,
Nor heard nor heeded groan and yell,
Some hellish spirit by him strode,
As, breathing slaughters out, he rode,

And through the spearmen's dense array
Towards the hangman clave his way;
Then seized the flaming torch he bore,
And drove it down through teeth and jaw.
So Lancelot to Guinevra came,
And on his charger placed the dame;
Then, gathering round him all his force,
Exultant, homeward turned his horse.

  Oh, day of mourning! Day of woe!
When many a guiltless head lay low.
And they, too, lay there, pale and red,
Those gentle children—all were dead;
And hideous still was seen the blow
Of horse's hoof on breast and brow.
A cry might rend a heart in twain
Brought forth King Arthur and Gawain.
Ah! well might hero's cheek turn pale
At such unutterable bale!
He pressed his ear against their heart,
Their closèd eyelids forced apart;

But from their eyes the light was fled,
And at their hearts the sound was staid.
Then, like a lioness roaring o'er
The bleeding head of whelps she bore,
In sorrow's deadly-stifled tone
His breast gave utterance to its moan :
'Light of my eyes! my joy, my pride!
Why did I let you from my side?
What to your mother shall I say?
Oh! would that by your side I lay!
For, now truth's fearful light I view,
This doom upon myself I drew!
I know too well that I have been
His comrade, partner in his sin;
I saw my emperor beguiled,
His honour and his fame defiled,
And conscience' voice I heard no more,
To friendship faithful as I swore.
And this the guerdon that I gain—
A heart's long night of endless pain.

The wolf your tender life had spared,
Nor deed so false, so foul had dared,—
But with his ruthless, cursèd arm,
He did not fear to do you harm!
The snake had felt some pity rise
At sight of your beseeching eyes;
Your eyes—whom blind and deaf he thrust
Beneath his charger in the dust!
So now, by hell's infernal gate,
I swear with him eternal hate!
Yes, though my heart should faint in death,
My hate shall still sustain my breath;
But when I weary of the strife—
That be my latest hour of life!'

 The warrior rose, to fury fanned,
And seized in wrath the monarch's hand:
'Swear me, Sir Emperor, as I swore,
With Lancelot eternal war,
Unceasing, ruthless, till I say
Myself that peace your hand may stay.

'T was hate that hurled the dreadful word
Which Arthur's heart responsive heard;
For deep within him burned the flame
Of hate, revenge, and conscious shame.
So thought and feeling he forsook,
And heedless that great oath he took.

V.

On Joyeuse Garde, within the fort,
This night unwonted guests were brought—
To that strong tower of safety came
The warrior with the lovely dame.
There, from the loftiest chamber, she
Gazed sad and silent on the sea,
Whose waves, that wildly leaped and reared,
Less stormy than her breast appeared.
And nought she ate, and nought she drank,
And her eye with watching sorely sank.
Three weary days she watched and wept,
And her soul's great anguish never slept.
The warrior, filled with love's alarms,
More closely held her in his arms:
He prayed—she heard not; he caressed—
She heeded not the hand that pressed.

She heard nought, felt nought, as the shore
Nor feels nor hears the breakers roar.
Then low his head Sir Lancelot bow'd,
And hid his face and wept aloud:
' Alas! the day that I was born,
The light that cheered my life is gone!
The love that I for many a year
Beheld by day, in dreams appear,
Which with it thousand sorrows brought,
For which a thousand fights I fought—
The love I sued from Death and won,
Is now for ever dead and gone!'

Then shed the dawning beams of day
Upon her face a quickening ray;
Then from her heart there burst a sigh,
And low and sad was her reply:
'O would that I had yesterday
In dust and ashes passed away.
Behind me light and glory lie:
Oh, why not rather let me die?

For now my heart had been at rest—
Love, guilt, and shame no more oppressed.
I had atoned—the fiercest foe
Had shed a tear upon my woe.
Atoned, forgiven, now can be
No more the blood you shed for me!
My life was forfeit—now, far worse,
Men hold it hardly worth a curse.
Oh! gaze not, gaze not on me so—
Release me, quit, renounce, forego!
You saved me—are you planning now
New shame for my poor burning brow?
I loved you once, my Lancelot;
But, oh! whom now I love—God wot.
Here, in your house, I dare not stay—
I go upon my lone, dark way.
Oh take, no more with me to play,
Those merciless dear hands away!
Remote from thine my future flies—
There is a sword between us lies.'

In wistful agony he raised
His eye, and sadly on her gazed.
In that dumb anguish well he knows
That earth hath gathered all its woes;
He feels that there is that must sever
His heart, his life from hers for ever,
As from the shipwrecked's straining eyes
Night hides the shore where dear hope lies.
He sinks his head upon her knee,
And weeps and weepeth bitterly.

An hour he lay, when on his ear
There thundered, from the valley near,
The tramp of hoofs, the trumpet's clang,
While spear and shield their music rang;
Dark horsemen in their battle-pride,
Along the still green valley ride.
A bloodier tournay this, I ween,
Than that at Camalot had been.

Then fiercely rose Sir Lancelot,
And on his shield a blow he smote;

His banner felt the morning's breath,
He thought of, and he longed for death.
With flashing steel, with hearts of oak,
To battle hied his warrior folk.

Ho! glorious morning for the fray!
Spring rains its blossoms on the way.
The breeze is cool, the sky is blue,
On helm and harness flashes dew;
The snorting horses, as they wheel,
Neigh answer to the trumpet's peal;
With brandished swords are seen among
The trees a wild impetuous throng;
Their cheeks a-glow, hearts beating high,
In wild desire to do or die.

Oh, where can death so fair be found
As on the soft, sweet forest-ground?
Where murmuring streamlets, cool and deep,
Shall sing the warriors' hearts to sleep;
The lark raise round them, as they die,
His glorious hymn of victory.

See on the field Sir Lancelot ride,
With many a hero at his side!
Brave young Sir Lyonel was there—
A joyous youth, serene and fair,
From that strange, peaceful fable-land
He came, from Brittany's green strand.
With deep, rough voice, an uncouth song
Sang Bohort as he rode along:
A rough old blade was he, and feared—
His hair was white and red his beard;
From his Carmarthen forests came
The bristly boar-skin round his frame,
Which, with the rusty helm he bore,
Was all the harness that he wore.
A small, long-handled hammer placed,
Like some toy plaything, at his waist,
With mighty spear, and slender shield,
He trots defiant through the field.

Then tramping hoof and clashing spear
Made music on the soldier's ear.

Loud rang the coats of mail,
Sharp arrows fell like hail;
And many a knight from his proud selle
On the trod grass death-rattling fell.
But in the loudest of the storm,
There ever rose Sir Lancelot's form;
And everywhere before his thrust
The foemen scattered like the dust.
One only in the hostile line
He shuns—his friend in arms, Gawain,—
Who madly presses through the throng,
And follows Lancelot along;
But swifter, in that fearful fray
Sir Lancelot ever steals away.
His presence now he will not brook,
He dares not in his eyes to look;
He knows that bloody deed of his
Cost Gawain his life's happiness.

But meanwhile Bohort, at his side,
Set out upon his ghastly ride.

Before the hammer that he wielded
The stoutest joint of harness yielded;
Visor and helm no more availed,
Nor shield nor armour trebly mailed;
And even those he scarcely touched
Were soon in endless slumber couched.
'Come, heavy-laden and opprest,'
He cried, 'and I will give you rest!
I'll ease the burden of your woe,
The road to Heaven I will show.'
Sir Lancelot cried, 'Old Shaggy-beard,
Was ever such a Saviour heard!
Methinks the lessons you have read
Are somewhat hard for human head.'

And swifter rain the blows, I ween,
A bloodier May-day ne'er was seen.
Began to yield the king's proud host,
When Arthur, seeing all was lost,
Grasped his huge spear, and spurred along
In wild haste through the fighting throng.

'Hey!' cried Bohort, and grasped his spear,
'The cock of all the walk comes here!'
'Keep off, keep off,' spake Lancelot,
'And scorn the good old emperor not!'
But he his lance couched in reply—
'No pardon shall he find for this,
That to avenge a woman's kiss
So many warriors here must die.'
He spurred his charger, couched his lance,
And darted on the king at once.
The shock that followed clave in twain
Old Bohort's shield—but Arthur, pale
And fiercely wounded through his mail,
Sank slowly on the gory plain.
Then Bohort shouted his wild song
Of victory, and stormed along;
And after him the horsemen rode,
And ranks of foemen down they trod;
Until not one before them stood,
But all flew fighting through the wood.

Sir Gawain covered the retreat,
And Bohort shouted in pursuit.

But meanwhile, straightway to the spot
Where fell the king rode Lancelot,
And deeply then men heard him moan:
'That eye of mine should gaze upon
The king, my lord, who knighted me,
Struck down to earth so wrongfully!'
He springs from horse, and bends him o'er
The gray old monarch wounded sore;
Chooses a sunny spot of ground,
Pours healing balm upon his wound,
And soothes the burning pain, and stays
The blood with soft, cool bandages;
Brings his own horse, and leads the way
To Joyeuse Garde from that grim fray.
'Come, sire, with me. About the wood
Your people manfully have stood;
But you shall find on Joyeuse Garde
The rest you need, and watch and ward.

But not as prisoner,—no, no,—
As lord and monarch you shall go;
And I, and all upon my lands
Are vassals, sire, to your commands.'
The monarch heard but half his words,
And wonderingly looked towards
Sir Lancelot, who raised his face
With eye so truthful in its gaze,
That Authur felt a gentle smart
Of sorrow on his aged heart,
And thought how fond in times now gone,
How glad on him those eyes had shone,
He feels a tear about his eye,
His bosom scarce restrains a sigh.
'Woe!' said the hoary, wounded man,
'That ever this foul war began.'
He sank back into thought at last,
Nor marked the blossoms blowing past,
Nor breezes whispering round him mild,
But followed silent, like a child.

So sat there till his failing force
Quite left him; then, the noble horse
Sir Lancelot silent led toward
The rocky crags of Joyeuse Garde.

High up ascends the mountain pass,
Green lies beneath the sunny grass,
In silence that the broadsword's stroke,
Like bells afar off chiming, broke.

On Joyeuse Garde hath found the guest,
In quiet chamber, care, and rest.
On a soft pillow there he lay,
And passed in wild dreams many a day.
There, in that twilight, Death and Life
About his pillow waged their strife.
A tender hand he feels assuage
And cool the fever's scorching rage;
And often, as he lifts his head,
Half dreams—half sees about his bed
A lovely woman stand, and two
Large eyes gaze on him, soft and blue.

He fancies, in some tale he read,
The lovely woman at his bed
Had once been all his own—and then
Sleep closes down his eyes again.
Hour after hour beside his bed
She sat, and not a word she said;
But ministering hand and eye,
Her wounded lord's least want supply.
So passed the night and came the morrow,
And still her eyes are wake for sorrow:
She sat alone, nor ceased to scan
That old, that sorely wounded man!
' Sure once his features were not quite
So pale, his hair so snowy white?'
She knows too well 't is grief defines
So deeply round his mouth the lines;
But darker in her soul it grows,
As he, in dream, towards her bows,
As if once more to rest upon her
The head she robbed of peace and honour.

As fixed on him her eye remains,
And sorrow beats with stormy pains,
Bursts from her heart asunder
The chain that long hath bound her;
As after sultry hours the rain
Falls richly on the thirsty plain,—
So down her face and o'er her limbs
Descend the heavy tears in streams.
And close by Arthur, on his bed,
She, sobbing, lays her golden head:
Her heart is lightened, filled with peace,
And all her woes in slumber cease.

O Fate, thy ways are strange and deep!
Now calmly side by side they sleep;
It was but glory's fatal glare
In union brought this ill-matched pair,
Now crushed by sorrow and opprest,
As if in mockery, they rest—
A wounded heart, a wounded head,
On sorrow's burning marriage-bed.

Sir Lancelot is wake betimes,
And softly to that chamber climbs;
But well his steps might pause in awe,
And wonder at the sight he saw :
He gazed in half unconscious stare
At those pale sleepers slumbering there.
Felt slowly the fierce pain depart,
And pride and shame creep o'er his heart,
Bowed in submission to his doom,
And softly turned to leave the room.

  Again the sun all silently
Rose glorious from the purple sea.
Exulting in its own bright ray,
It casts abroad the sparks of day;
And from yon heaven's blue loneliness
It passes o'er a world's distress.
And land and ocean shout aloud,
And all earth's strangely varied crowd;
The eagle soars through clouds aglow,
The fish leaps from clear waves below,

And from the forest's golden bower,
Their song a thousand voices shower;
The bells of morning chime out clear
Their music on the traveller's ear.

    The lark's glad note, the beam of day,
Broke on the room where Arthur lay;
The hum of life he heard around,
And looked up, wondering at the sound.
Out of that fever, sleep and night,
His spirit wakes, serene and bright;
He feels the power of health that rains
Its quickening life through all his veins.
But all he saw seemed wondrous strange,
As he let his eye about him range.
Beside him lay a woman there,
Whose soft fine hand, whose golden hair,
Seem known to him: a neck like this,
And this imperial form—it is,
It is his own poor Guinevere.
The lovely dame he saw appear

In that wild dream of his was, then,
No fancy of a fevered brain.
At once some magic seems to raise
A vision of the last sad days:
Then of that burning stake he thought—
Thought how she fled, and how they fought;
How hard a bed old Bohort gave,
And how Sir Lancelot came to save.
In depth of anguish then he raised
Himself, and fondly on her gazed.
'T was she who watched her health away,
To wait upon him night and day;
To wait on him, at whose command
They gave her in the hangman's hand.
Her face is pale and weary yet,
Her eye is red, the pillow wet:
' In her great anguish, as I slept,
In silence for us both she wept.
O if that I had never seen
Thee, then not such thy lot had been!

My folly dearly I must rue,
And joyless now is all I do :
Deep in my heart that blow I feel—
The wounds of honour who can heal?
By heaven! Thy guilt was great indeed—
Now greater, painfuller thy need.
Those tears of thine can still subdue
My heart, and cause it weep for you.
But all is lost, and we must go
Each on our lonely path of woe.
Sleep on—our joys, our woes are cast
Beneath the shadows of the past;
In the new life from now I live,
All that is over I forgive.'

As long he sat in earnest thought,
His ear approaching voices caught;
The tread of men the silence breaks,
And Guinevere at length awakes.
There comes a gold-haired youth, to bring
Keys, huge and heavy, to the king.

'Sir King, your life by God be blessed!
We do Sir Lancelot's behest.
This morning he, with all his host,
Set sail for ever from this coast.
These are the keys of Joyeuse Garde,
He sends back to his feudal lord.'

The king was silent and amazed,
Guinevra through the window gazed:
Three vessels, each a distant star,
Upon the ocean flashed afar;
But not a motion could one trace
Of feeling on Guinevra's face.
Then spake the monarch: 'Come with me,
My guardian care rest over thee!
But thou art free—I ask not now
Obedience to the marriage vow,
But thou shalt be my child, and I
Will guard thy peace with watchful eye.
And now, forgotten be the past,
Forgotten long as life shall last.

I may not love thee, cannot hate,—
Trust only, I will not forsake!'
He spake, and gazed in earnest mood
Upon her—bathed in tears she stood—
Turned not her face upon her lord,
But gave her hand, without a word.

VI.

'Speak not of peace!' exclaimed Gawain;
'My lords, my lords, the war is mine.
Four spirits stand by night and cry
About my bed-side suppliantly:
" Why dost thou rest, Gawain, Gawain?
What did'st thou swear, Gawain, Gawain? '
These ghostly words shall ring and ring
For ever in your ears, Sir King.
Touched by Guinevra's woful pain,
You chose to take her home again;
And peace be with her; but you swore
With Lancelot eternal war!
I sought him madly in that fray,
But cowardly he stole away
And fled; but over sea and land
I'll follow, to earth's furthest strand.

And you, my lords, ye lead not home
Your armies, but with me ye come:
By Him who perjury will not brook,
Remember that great oath ye took.
Yes, noble sirs, I see you here
Impatient wielding sword and spear;
I see your vengeful eyebrows lower
Impatient of the battle hour.
The first fight we, for vengeance, fought,
Defeat and shame upon us brought,
And now, by heaven, who shall dare
To speak of respite from the war?
Stand side by side courageously!
The foe has fled to Brittany:
Tho' tempests toss the stormy main,
Hoist sail and at him now again!'

Then clashed together sword and shield,
War-cries resounded through the field.
This swung his axe, and that his lance,
In sunshine plume and pennon dance.

The monarch saw that his command
Was given to a stranger's hand,
And to his passion vent he gave:
'Aye, rule! and I will be your slave'—
Then checked himself at once, and spoke:
'Who says that I my fealty broke?
You wanted war—war you shall have—
Let them that fall not dig our grave.'
Then all those warriors shouted, 'War!'
One only sat there and forbore
All utterance—Mordred—who of old
Was silent, dark, reserved, and cold.
He presses his pale lips together,
His eyes and lids are red with fever,
And on his shaven head there stand
The tokens of Sir Lancelot's hand;
The sick man on his bed they bore,
To give his counsel on the war.

There, sighing deeply as he lay,
He looked on war's confused array:

'Alas!' he cried, 'that I, sick man,
Not to the battle hasten can!
Gawain, thy face is bright with glee;
How gladly were I now with thee!
While I lie groaning, thou can'st go
And wreak thy vengeance on our foe;
Can'st seek him, and thine anger sate
In blows, while I can only hate.'

   That moment Arthur, on his throne,
Addressed him: 'Thou, my sister's son,
Must stay behind; and to thy hand
I give my people and my land—
My honour and my rule uphold,
Until the days of war be told.'
Then Mordred bowed, 'I trust ere long,
Sir King, to join that warrior throng.'
'Be wise, be wise,' the king replied,
'Enough of us to battle ride.
Can Hope suggest thee ought more grand
Than Britain's sceptre in thy hand?

My country's guardian power to be,
I know that I have none like thee.'

And meanwhile, in the summer sun,
The toil and labour have begun.
And ships, that idle long have lain,
Are once more rocking on the main;
And once again the sound is heard
Of jarring boom, and creaking yard;
And flag and pennant stream out bright
With bars and crosses—red and white.
And Arthur's purple standard, fair
With thirteen crowns, is waving there.
From ship to ship, the file and rank
Are marched upon the gangway plank;
The sailors hurrying to and fro
Find work enough for each to do,
In clearing tackle, rope, and cord,
Or leading plunging steeds aboard.
Ashore the clashing weapons ring,
And sailors shout and soldiers sing;

While, sad at heart, amid that loud
Confusion, pale-faced women crowd.
A wife the rider's bridle grasped,
A sobbing boy his stirrup clasped;
Some archer fondly took aside,
To kiss once more, his weeping bride;
Some hoary warrior, in his tent,
His son to war with blessings sent;
Some mother, from the castle tower,
Gazed mournful on the sons she bore;
The hand of friend was clasped by friend—
It seemed that parting ne'er would end.

But up and off! to sea they go!
The bellying sails gleam white as snow,
The waters foam beneath the keel,
While loud the sailors' voices peal:

'We love thee, green and glorious sea,
Earth's ancient mother, wild and free!
By grief, by woe, no more opprest,
Thou rockest on thy waves to rest,

With hoarse but mighty tones,
Britannia's valiant sons.

A mighty warrior guides our helm,
Before us lies the world—our realm.
For in the hollow of thy hand
Thou holdest earth's remotest strand.
Those only dear to thee
Earth's emperors shall be.'

Then soon upon the course they steer,
The coasts of Brittany appear;
And through the waves that break and roar
They fight each footstep to the shore.
No more on Lancelot, no more,
In fortune smiles the star of war;
No more his followers can oppose
Th' o'erwhelming numbers of their foes.
So, weary to the death, he falls
Back within Benwic's loyal walls.

Before those ramparts many a day,
The king's beleaguering army lay,—
Upon the wall, and in the moat,
Right deadly was the fight they fought.
And six moons waxed and six moons waned,
While Arthur little vantage gained.
Then Gawain rode, in harnessed state,
At dawn, before the city gate,
And cried, 'Now meet me, Lancelot,
Thou murderer, if thou fear'st me not!'
But Lancelot, who sat at meat,
With all his people kept his seat;
And as he hearkened Gawain cry,
A cloud of sorrow dimmed his eye:
'In love these eyes no more shall gaze
Upon my friend in happier days.
I mourn the crimes that sever
Me from Gawain for ever.
But now, my warriors, seated here,
I charge you, as my wrath ye fear,

Before the gate let no one ride
To meet him, though he thus defied.'
Each head, in all that warlike crowd,
In token of obedience bowed,
And Gawain called aloud in vain;
Then, angry, sought his tent again.
And every morning at the gate,
Defiant on his steed he sat;
But silence gave in Lancelot's hall
Mute answer to his furious call.

But meanwhile, never Lancelot
His lovely Guinevere forgot,
And mightier still the longing grew
Her sunny face and form to view.
For love at least—if love alone—
His heart might dare to call its own.
Love, freed from every wild desire—
Love, purified in painful fire.
But anguish bowed his haughty head—
To him she was for ever dead.

His future lay out dark and dim,
And hope itself was pain to him.
Like some pale dreamer, wandered he
About his castle moodily:
One word from that dear mouth might give
His thirsting heart new strength to live:
'Poor fool,' he whispered, ' to delude
Thy heart with lies that do no good!
Be still, my heart, be still, 't is vain;
Thou ne'er canst see her face again!'

So mused he once about the hour,
Of sunrise on the castle tower.
His eye, with grief and watching worn,
Gazed vacant on the rising morn;
He hears the lark's clear note, the dove
Not far off coos its tale of love;
His feet on trampled roses seem
To tread, in his half-waking dream.
Then Bohort came, and shook his head,
That rough, true warrior, as he said:

'What ails you, master? whither fled
From your fair cheeks the rosy red?
Tears are for women; do you deem
Their traces eyes like yours beseem!
Speak out—your hand upon your heart—
Confess you feel that love still smart.
Indeed I pity you, else I would—
By heavens—speak in other mood!
I, too, was young—that I can say—
But things were different in my day.
I, too, a maiden's hand have pressed—
Looked, curious, on a maiden's breast;
But lovesick, by my gray old hair,
I never was—*that* I can swear.
Shame, shame, for you to pine away,
And joy no more in fight and fray.
See, in bright armour at the gate
Sir Gawain rides, to vent his hate
Upon you, scorn you, and defy;
Shake off your love-sick lethargy,

Sir Gawain's body soundly hammer,
And stop this brawler's noisy clamour.'

  Gawain the gate's broad portal smote,
And called aloud to Lancelot:
' I greet thee with my curse each day,
Why, reptile, hide thyself away?
To mortal combat I defy
Thee—thou didst love the battle-cry;
But children are a fitter aim
For arms of one so lost to shame.
Thou dar'st not meet a brave man's gaze:
Hide, coward, hide thy foul disgrace !
Jest of the world, poor Lancelot,
Who cares if thou art slain or not?
Sure death can only gain appear,
So lay aside thine abject fear !
Conceal thy face 'neath visor well—
And let me speed thy soul to hell.'

  For all old Bohort's frowning face,
Sir Lancelot stirred not from his place,

But gazed with dark and moody eyes.
Then Bohort felt his fury rise;
The wind blew his rough beard about,
He shook his fist, and shouted out:
'You sit and hear that scorn of his,—
By God, *I*'ll punish him for this!
Where is my horse? and where my lance?
I'll stop his cursed mouth at once.'
Then Bohort, with a mighty roar,
Stormed down the stairway of the tower,
And vainly beckoned Lancelot,
Who heard full soon the charger trot,
With echoing tramp through yard and gate,
To the free space where Gawain sate.

As Gawain recognised the shout
Of Bohort, his fierce heart laughed out:
Through vexing hours he long had sought
A foeman, and there rode Bohort;
Beneath whose blows on that sad day
His prince, imperial Arthur, lay.

His stature to its height he dressed,
And laid, like lightning, lance in rest.
The rage, the scorn, the hate he feels,
With giant strength his body steels.
He darted on Bohort at once,
And laid so mightily his lance,
That from firm and fixèd selle,
Each of those twain warriors fell.
Gawain his feet full quickly gained,
But Bohort rolled upon the sand:
So fierce the blow that Gawain gave,
Thro' shield, thro' breast and back it clave.
Wrestling with death, brief space he knelt,
His hammer still more tightly held,
Then bowed his head, and fell again,
A quivering corse upon the plain;
And all the ground with blood was red:
So that rough soldier lay there, dead!

 Then from the rampart walls about,
A clamour fierce and wild broke out.

Upon the roof, to Lancelot hied
His knights, and loud for vengeance cried.
But Lancelot's wild eyes remain
Fixed sadly on the fatal plain :
'Oh ! that the truest man of all,
The bravest here for me should fall ! '
And, as he cried, awoke once more
Th' heroic rage of days of yore.
Once more his nodding plume he took,
And fiercely on his helm it shook ;
He girded swift, without a word,
About his thigh his mighty sword ;
Fixed lance in rest, and loosening rein,
He galloped out upon the plain.

Fierce was the combat of that hour.
As in a heavy April shower
Great raindrops pour down rattling, so
Fell loudly rattling blow on blow ;
And every stroke that either bore,
Did honour to their school of war.

Right swift, right strong they smote, they clave,
Their harness sparks of red fire gave,
As stroke on stroke their broadswords drave.
Both armies stood and marked from far
The combat of these chiefs of war;
And rough old soldiers laughed, and swore
Such fight was never seen before.
High in his stirrup, Lancelot,
Through Gawain's shield and bridle smote:
So true the blow he struck, so well,
That Gawain's charger reared and fell.
Then sprang Sir Lancelot to the ground,
And scarcely had firm footing found,
When Gawain, raging, at him ran,
And angrier yet the fight began.
Then the good steel in splinters flew,
And blood streamed all their armour through.
Till Lancelot in fury sped
So stern a dint on Gawain's head,
That through his helmet, bruised and crushed,
A stream of hot, clear life-blood gushed;

And Gawain sank, beside his horse,
Upon the field—a senseless corse.
　Sir Lancelot bowed his weary head,
His bosom heaved, his strength was fled;
Scarce consciously he looked upon
The deed of blood that he had done.
And, as he stood there long and gazed,
His wounded head that other raised:
Bewildered, through his bleeding eyes,
He saw Sir Lancelot, and with sighs
And groans, and gnashing teeth he spake,
In hatred that not death could slake:
'Strike! it is shame my life should stand
In peril of thy murderous hand!'
But Lancelot answered, 'Oh, Gawain,
Think thou wast once dear friend of mine!
Oh, let our strife be ended now!
I feel the debt to thee I owe,
And little I should care to live,
If but my death to thee could give

What, to my own great agony,
For madness blind I stole from thee.
But let the past's sad memories cease:
Gawain, I freely offer peace!'
That other clenched, with bloody hand,
And cast on Lancelot the sand:
'Be still! speak not of peace to me:
Strike, that thy face no more I see,—
Thy hated face,—then flee away;
And dare not by my side to stay,
Lest, by thy presence here opprest,
My spirit should refuse to rest.
Through the dark vale I'll gladly go,
But ask for mercy of thee!—No!
Said Lancelot, 'God keep thee, since
Thou wilt not peace,'—so turned him thence.
But Gawain, mad with pain and wrath,
Drew from his side the dagger forth,
His splintered harness forced apart,
And drove it fiercely through his heart.

Swift from the wound the blade he drew,
And madly at Sir Lancelot threw:
' Far better to my grave be brought,
Than owe thee, caitiff, thanks for aught.'

  Sir Lancelot stood and held his breath,
While Gawain's wild eyes closed in death ;
Then turned him sad and silent round,
And left pale Gawain on the ground.
So came a bloody peace, to end
This mortal feud 'twixt friend and friend.

VII.

But Mordred ruled, with guardian hand,
The Britons' green and sunny land.
To Camalot, where he held his court,
Right kingly was the pomp he brought,
And lord and villain, knight and knave,
Approved the equal laws he gave.

Afar from halls of feast and state,
King Arthur's dame in sorrow sate,
And only memory came awhile
The silent moments to beguile;
As from her turret-cell the queen
Gazed pensive on the verdant scene,
And, in the sunny hours that flew,
The healing of Nepenthe drew.

Her casement's arching ivy made
A temple, to whose ample shade

Oft finch, or dove, or swallow came—
The welcome guests of that high dame.

  Dark Mordred gladly kept aloof,
Nor loved to be beneath that roof.
Since that dread night he would not raise
His eyes to meet Guinevra's gaze.
For Mordred had no love-sick soul
Round a lost world of love to roll;
But hatred glowed through all his frame
At memory of Guinevra's shame.
Her sorrow seemed to him disguise,—
Her tears, her penitence, but lies.
But on a sultry summer day,
While sleep on field and castle lay,
He met Guinevra walking through
The garden's shadiest avenue.
She wore no ring upon her hand,
About her head no jewelled band,
But round a face like lily fair
Lay golden locks of waving hair.

And wondrous noble was the glance
And glory of her countenance:
The height of love she had secured,
And then its darkest death endured;
Her griefs were dead, her joys were done,
But round her still their glories shone;
And softened now the eye might trace
Their tokens on her earnest face.
Now calmly she could look upon
The desert of a life undone,
While sorrow round her golden head
All its majestic halo shed.

And Mordred reddening, pale in turn,
No longer felt that hatred burn.
She seemed not now as when, before,
The pomps of festal robes she bore,
When diamonds flashed and stars of gold
Beneath her veil's transparent fold.
He stood aside, half vacantly,
And mutely watched her passing by;

She gave one silent look to greet,
He bowed his forehead to his feet.

   Conflicting were the thoughts that prest
Through Mordred's proud, defiant breast;
He finds it fruitless now to blame
A feeling that he cannot tame.
He deems that hatred he conceived
The injustice of a heart deceived;
What though some feelings may rebel,
That form his reverence must compel.
So proud impatience urged him on,
And justice seemed to bid atone.
Where e'er he passed, on hill or lea,
Her chiding form he seemed to see.

   Nor meet he thought it she should dwell
A prisoner in that lonely cell,
But he, who till this year ignored
Himself the meaning of that word,
Determined now that Arthur's wife
Should be again restored to life;

So bade her ladies wait once more
Upon their mistress as before;
And welcome soon became to her
Their merry talk and tender care,
Though her long loneliness had made
At first Guinevra half afraid..
At noontide in the garden's bowers
They met to pass the sultry hours,
And many a merry jest and word,
And song and music oft were heard.

  But Mordred often came that way,
And well he loved with them to stay;
Nor left them soon, but hour by hour,
Stayed fettered by some unknown power:
'T was woman's sacred power could hold
Dominion o'er a man so bold.
It was Guinevra's countenance
Made his dark eye so brightly glance;
He saw nought, hearkened nought but her,
It was her beauty bound him there;

But not from pain his heart was free,
So poor, so wretched seemed to be
The things that once alone inspired,
The fortune once his heart desired.
And now he feels an unknown need—
A riddle this he cannot rede.

Thus once about the castle he
Was wandering in wild reverie;
Cool were the corridors and calm,
But in his head 't was sultry warm,
As through abandoned rooms he went,
Scarce consciously his steps he bent
To those remoter chambers, where
Of old had dwelt that lady fair.
What sudden vision saw he rise
To waken thus his dreaming eyes?
Within this chamber, breast to breast,
A happy pair once sank to rest:
And all was just as on that night,
When here they fought the dreadful fight.

The light that entered there was dim,
A stain of blood looked ghastly grim;
The carpet, thrown about the floor,
Some shreds of splintered armour bore;
Beside the bed the sunbeams shine
Upon a cup with dregs of wine;
The lamp was wet with oil which shone
That once too happy pair upon.
A fever through his body crept,
As Mordred to the bedside stept,
For in the linen tossed and strown
About the silken cushions thrown,
His eye perceives a hollow made
Where she her queenly body laid.
Then to his heart, in drunken flood,
Rushed every fountain of his blood;
And he who Nature's right foreswore,
Nor owned her sovereign power before,
Now, all undone, was called to prove
The Might, the Majesty of Love.

Before his fearless spirit swarm
Strange thoughts in fancy's wildest form—
The Night of Love has power to raise
Its strange eidolon to his gaze.
In vain he hurls it back, in vain—
In brighter hues it comes again;
And paints, to haunt his envious breast,
The joys his deadliest foe possessed.
As one to darkness born, and blind,
Who knew not that the world was kind,
Too long accustomed to the night,
He shuddered at the glorious light.
He grimly smiled, like one in pain,
Till his proud spirit rose again,
And fires of hate and flames of love
Burst out at once, his strength to prove,
Then with a shriek like one possessed,
He turned and fled in wild unrest.

  He came down to the airy hall
Where sat the ladies, joyous all.

A fountain murmured as it played,
A minstrel's harp sweet music made:

'My heart, my heart, if thou couldst dare,
  Were beauty's summit not too high,
'T were life indeed to live for her;
  Without her it were gain to die.
My heart, my heart, if thou couldst dare!

'Still! foolish love, and let me be:
  The sunshine of my days hath set,
Against all hope what hope for thee?
  No hope, no hope, but to forget;
Still! foolish love, and let me be!'.

No more could Mordred's heart contain
Its angry, long imprisoned pain.
He dashed the minstrel's harp away,
That shivered on the ground it lay:
'A coward song, a coward plaint,
For Love rhymed never with Restraint!

Were it not earthly, but divine,
By Heaven, this guerdon should be mine!'
So Mordred swore; but o'er him came
A sudden shock of maddening shame,
And but the fountain's warbling fall
Broke silence as he left the hall.

Then Mordred wandered forth alone,
While sunset's milder glories shone,
And over valley, mead, and glade,
The mountain summits cast their shade.
Half-murmured words of angry shame
From his contracted lips there came;
And fast and faster as he pressed—
Still faster beat his heart's unrest.
Around him evening's insects flew
As near a mighty stream he drew;
He sprang into the waves, that bore
Him coldly to the further shore—
Nor rested, but with swifter stride
He climbed the rocky, steep hill side;

And reached the dense pine-forest there,
As evening shed its latest glare.
  'Mid those primeval trees around,
The ear could catch no human sound,
But knotty branches creaked and groaned,
And owls their lonely music droned.
Through the drenched garments Mordred wore,
The wind came whistling from the shore,
But well it soothed his heart's disease,
To vex his body and displease.
Then through the darkness round about,
Two large gray eyes flashed fiercely out:
Dragging the carcase of an owl,
A wolf sprang forth, with angry howl,
Who, scenting Mordred as he stood,
Leapt on him with a rage for blood.
He, grimly glad to be provoked,
Grasped the huge creature, till he choked
Its life out, then he flung aside
The monster, quivering as it died.

But Mordred climbed on, restless still,
Towards the summit of the hill;
There sat him on a mossy stone,
In the cold moonshine, fiercely lone,
And breathed out curses through the night,
Like war-cries in the roar of fight.

'Thou wind, that from the tempest-cloud,
In terror movest, wild and loud;
Decked in thy cloudy garments grand,
Thou spreadest fear o'er sea and land!
The night-bird shrieks thy path before,
And forests groan, and waters roar;
The distant darkness feels thy hand,
Thou ragest free of all command.
A woman's sinful beauties hold
Me powerless in their guilty fold.
Before me ruin stands, while I
Nor care to live nor dare to die.
I know no feeling but desire—
I think of her, with veins on fire—

My conscience—all the prayers I say
Are smoke that vanishes away.
In vain, in vain has been the strife,
The work, the labours of my life.
I feel my boasted strength too slight
When passion calls her powers to fight.
Oh! might some flash from heaven descend,
And let my soul's oppression end!
That I my scorchèd heart might lave
For ever in the cold, cold grave!
Ah, no! that cursed, dear form I see,
That through the darkness beckons me;
And calls me, from my lonely woe,
Through love's ecstatic joys to go.'

He sprang up fiercely; from his thigh
He tore and raised his sword on high:
'God's wrath! I hold her 'neath my hand,
And hell shall answer my command.
Arthur, thine hour hath struck—what friend
Shall weep one tear to mourn thine end?

The world shall jeer thee when I claim—
I, mightier far—thy throne, thy dame!
Ye powers of Night, that round my brow,
Your ghostly, shadowy phantoms bow—
That lurk about to weave a thread
Of curses close about my head—
To you I consecrate this land,
This season, with my lifted hand!
Let horrors yet unseen appear,
For I am one that shall not fear!'

Then sank in darkness moon and star,
And storm and tempest came from far—
And heavy clouds, in rain and hail,
Poured deluge o'er the darkened vale.

Guinevra, boding trouble, lay,
As dawned the morning, pale and gray;
For Mordred's conduct seemed to tell
Of feelings that she loves not well.
The garden now she sought no more,
Nor called her ladies as before,

But, undisturbed, preferred to dwell
Again within her lonely cell.

   And meanwhile, Mordred's people ride
About the land, on every side.
A life of mystery began
To weave itself about the man.
Again was seen the haughty trace
Of pride upon his bearded face;
Once more he walked, reserved and cold,
A type of chivalry, weirdly bold.

   War's iron music, and the clang
Of armour through the land now rang;
Loud voices now began to raise
Their war-like hymns in Mordred's praise.

   'Moon waxes after moon to wane,
And Arthur comes not home again!
Sure he and all 'neath his command
Have fallen in the stranger's land.
An idle fancy led him on
To leave his people and his throne.

If he still lives, he must be changed
From all our customs and estranged—
Then let him, since he chooses, stay
For ever from his land away!
A mighty warrior, praised in song,
Courteous in peace, in battle strong—
Let Mordred mount on Arthur's throne,
Since Arthur has resigned his own!'

With anxious eyes the people gazed
Towards the storm around them raised.
In Camalot's halls, before the camp,
Where horsemen ride and footmen tramp,
And weapons clash, and clarions ring,
A priestly hand crowned Mordred king.

The sun shone on the chamber where
Guinevra sat, serene and fair;
She thought of sorrows, strifes, and crimes,
The horrors of those olden times;
But peace is in her heart at last,
For all those stormy days are past.

No tale of Benwic ever came
To knowledge of the lovely dame;
Towards the home of her great lover
She sent no secret thoughts, to hover,
Like love's dear angels, round his head—
She thought of him as one long dead.

She felt a draught of cooler air—
'T was Mordred's form before her there.
Around his harnessed limbs there flowed
Rich folds of purple as he strode:
The golden hoop about his brow
Proclaimed him Britain's emperor now.
Before that eye's joy-burning black
She started, filled with horror, back.
He cried, 'Thou sunny face, essay
Not from me now to flee away!
That those dear eyes for me might roll,
I gladly forfeited my soul;
In hell's grim darkness I shall see
Their beauty beaming mild on me;

My mercy grants but brief delay,
For thou art mine, art mine this day.
I sit on poor old Arthur's throne—
For thou art fit for kings alone.
Be still, Guinevra! I am not—
By Heaven—worse than Lancelot!
Speak not of duty! look not so!
Thou dost not love me—that I know.
Of scorn and hatred thou may'st speak—
I'll kiss in love thine angry cheek.
Though but thy curses meet my ear,
My blessings only you shall hear!
For thou art mine, and shalt be mine,
Though earth and heaven their powers combine!
And when love's bloom shall fade away,
My heart with smiles shall die that day.'

 Astonished, scarce she dared to scan
The features of that fearful man:
Again the peace was hurled and cast
Away, that she had found at last;

Again in giant stature loom
Conceptions of her destined doom :
She sees in the surrounding night,
Confusion, murder, war and fight.
Then vainly she essayed to speak,
Tears streaming down her blanchèd cheek—
Saw only, sinking to the ground,
Fire flashing through the darkness round.
The crown of gold fell from his head
As Mordred clasped her, half afraid.
On high he raised the fallen dame,
Through door and portal swiftly came,
Through crowded halls he hurried on,
And laid her on the cushioned throne.
Her face, like marble, lies serene
Upon the velvet's purple sheen ;
The warrior stands to gaze in pride
Upon his pale yet beauteous bride ;
While joyful all his people sing,
'Hail, Mordred, Britain's chosen King !'

That Night, while men were feasting late,
A page stole through the castle gate:
With hurrying steps he passed along,
Inhospitable woods among.
Soft was the hand his sword that bore,
The thorns his garments rent and tore,—
'Twas Guinevere, with blood all red,
From her impetuous bridegroom fled.
She prayed Heaven's blessing as she strode,
Undaunted on that lone dark road;
The pain, the toil she deemed but slight,
Nor paused she once to rest that night.
At dawn to Almesbury cloister came,
Exhausted, faint, the luckless dame,
And in dark sanctuary remained,
By anxious fears oppressed and pained.

VIII.

In Arthur's camp, the gentle knight,
Gawain, was buried in the night.
Through the broad valley every tent
The lurid glare of torch-fire sent.
On open bier the corpse they bear,
A garland round the smooth long hair;
The bearers, with mute steps and slow,
In deathly still procession go;
Hoarse trumpets echo through the camp,
And iron hoofs in measured tramp;
The towers and walls of Benwic show
Black flags in funeral pomp that flow.

Peaceful and pleasant, in the wood
A chapel with its churchyard stood;
And here, beneath the oak-tree's shade,
The gallant warrior's corpse they laid.

As mutely dust to dust they gave,
Leaves sere and fading filled the grave;
While through autumnal forests round,
Began the dirge's mournful sound:

'Sleep on in holy rest, till dawn
The glories of the Unknown Morn!
'T was thine in early youth to prove
The pains of hate, the joys of love.
With honour still unsullied bright
Thou camest out of every fight.
Though love must fade and hate decay,
Thy name shall never pass away!'

In thoughtful mood stood Arthur there,
And gazed out through the morning air.
Above the far horizon came
The clouds of sunrise, fringed with flame.
He seemed in that red-rosy glow
The mysteries of the heavens to know;
And yonder, in those realms of blue,
He saw, in robes of dazzling hue,

Gawain, serenely splendid, stand,
His brothers holding either hand!
  So Gawain passed away in peace
To where the pains of hatred cease.

  The monarch left the camp's loud throng,
And rode in reverie along.
The air was cool, and silvery blue
Lay woods and meads, in dawn and dew:
Bright memories, faded long before,
Rose to the monarch's soul once more.
And on he rode, while fresh the wind
Blew through the wood of Brocelind.

  But faded soon the woods away,
And vale and mead before him lay;
Where all the joys of spring appear,
And fountains murmur cool and clear.
Here purple moth and gaudy fly
Their wings in beaming sunshine ply;
Here bees about the clover hum,
And all the air is filled with bloom,

That snow-white falls, from flowering trees,
On lilies and anemonies.

In wonder gazed the king around,
O'er all that fragrant, flowery ground;
His eyes he covered with his hand,
And thought himself in faëry land.
Dismounting, fresh he walked and hale,
That old man, through the magic vale;
Then, in a field of purple flower,
He saw a foliage-covered bower,
That, in fantastic form, had made
A tent beneath a thorn-tree's shade.
Within he saw a man, at rest
Upon a tall fair woman's breast.
Beneath a veil of gauzy green,
Some tokens of her form were seen;
She sang—half smiling, half in tears—
A wayward song of hopes and fears;
The birds, upon the branches round,
Sat wondering at the plaintive sound,

Whose rhythmic flections had a power
To shake and thrill the magic bower.
About her faëry face was shed
A circling light of rosy red.
Grand was the form of him who pressed
His knightly head against her breast:
His hair and beard, of ruddy gold,
Shone round a face serenely bold;
On those black eyes of his there lay
The radiance of no earthly day;
From every line his brow that seamed
A spiritual glory beamed.
Upon a visage pale as snow
Lay tokens of a hopeless woe,
Of hardly wrung restraint,
And love's unspoken plaint.
His eye gazed upward, dreamy-bright,
To those two hills of snowy white,
As, resting on her tender knees,
He hearkened those sweet melodies.

The king, in wonder, paused to scan
The well-known lineaments of the man:
'What, Merlin, dost thou reappear—
Unknown, unheard of many a year?
A thousand messengers I sent,
Who vainly went, and came, and went.
By what strange peradventure meet
We, in this forest's blest retreat?'
    Then Merlin raised, in glad surprise,
On Arthur his delighted eyes:
'What rich, dear memories appear,
As that lov'd voice once more I hear!
Long have I waited in desire
Of thee—my lord, imperial sire!
I who was life's impatient guest
Awhile, now here for ever rest;
I, earth and air too small who found,
Within this blooming bower am bound.
An adamant coffin holds me tight,
Its shape unseen to mortal sight.

These things—this faëry child, my swan,
My bird of plaintive song, hath done.
She weeps—all I shall ever know,
Is that she loveth, mourneth so.
The prince of darkness chose me, knight
On earth, and herald of his might—
He taught me his mysterious ken,
That I, a man, should ruin men.
This knowledge to the light I brought,
That so his schemes were turned to nought;
He planned my ruin from that hour,
And forged a word of dreadful power,
That, spoken, all my strength should hold
In an inextricable fold.
So, in the woods of Brocelind,
Fair Vivian 't was my doom to find;
And soon to the enchantress gave
My heart, my thoughts, a willing slave.
Fooled by one kiss of that sweet lip,
My mouth the fatal word let slip.

She is a woman : so she spake
The word, and nought on earth can break—
No sighs, no tears—the magic chain
Within whose links I must remain.
Old as the ancient shades of night,
Is this dark incantation's might;
Strong as the fastnesses of hell,
And merciless as death its spell.'

Then Vivian's hands, convulsive, prest
His lips against her yielding breast;
She drank the tears that down her cheeks
Their tokens left in frequent streaks;
And raised great eyes of blue to scan
The features of the foreign man.

'Ah! woe is thee!' great Arthur cried,
And heaved his breast, and deeply sighed.
Then Merlin raised prophetic eyes:
'Cry woe upon thyself—low lies
Thy greatness, all crushed out between
The clasping arms of thy frail queen.

Her beauty wove its chains and bound
Thy heroes of the Table Round.
Now cast thy sword-sheath in the sea—
Lead home thy hosts, and let them be
For deeds of blood arrayed,
For Mordred hath betrayed!
Betrayed—to touch thy consort's hand—
Thyself, thy people, and thy land.
Mid sounds of revel, on my ear
Strike murder, war—and silent fear!
Arthur, farewell—those days are told,
Those glorious, knightly days of old,
And new-born generations bloom
About the graves that mark your doom.
But over death exalted, I
Here, here for ever buried, lie!'

   Then twilight lowered around, and shed
Green shadows o'er his fallen head,
Like tones of flute or silver bell
The faëry maiden's music fell.

She sings of nights when lovers rest,
Enamoured, sleepless, breast to breast;
Of beings blest, who round dear charms
In rapture glue their clasping arms.
But, through her thoughts of pleasure, flows
A whole eternity of woes.
There falls, from those great eyes of blue,
Upon her breast a pearly dew,
That trickles, from the roses there,
Down o'er her lover's golden hair.

Then rose a vapour grey and pale,
That hid in mist the verdant vale;
The music died, no sunbeams shone,
As Arthur stood there all alone;
And marked the ravens as they flew
The leafless, wintry forest through.

Falsehood, thou firstborn child of Night,
Enticing from their homes of light
Heaven's fairest Cherubim, that so
They sank in wastes of endless woe,

Embittering concord, poisoning peace,
Thou madest all earth's union cease.
Flames of thy kindling did destroy
The ancient temple-walls of Troy;
It was inspired by thy command,
That Hagen raised his murderous hand.
Some star of fortune must have dawned,
To spare him pains all else have mourned;
Whose heart had never yet to feel
Thy chilling breath, thy piercing steel.

 The king stood lost in all his fears,
His heart was drunk with rage and tears.
Though still that painful wound he felt,
Which those he loved so well had dealt,
He hoped that war and hate might cease,
Himself at length might part in peace.—
And now his sister's treacherous son
Had robbed him of his realm, his throne;
And Britain's people, and the land
He loved, upheld the traitor's hand.

Once more he felt his heart could blaze
With anger, as in younger days;
Serene his brow and glorious beamed,
New strength through all his stature streamed:
' If I am destined to forego
The peaceful days old age should know,'
He cried aloud, with flashing eye,—
' At least in battle I will die,
And meetly end, a grey-haired man,
The life a hero-child began ! '

He ran out of the withering wood,
And, as above the camp he stood,
Cried, ' Strike your tents without delay—
Our banners raise—we haste away !
No need on foreign wars to roam,—
There 's work enough for us at home.'

Resounded then the stirring camp
With noisy stroke and clamorous tramp;
Soon all was ready, and the gale
Filled rudely every bellying sail,

And through rough seas that mighty force
Sailed homeward on its northward course.

Thou traitor to thy fathers' land,
See, Mordred, lour the vengers' hand.
The vulture looks for food once more,
The wolves of Wales are at the door,
They snuff and scent blood in the air—
Snow-King, Snow-King, beware, beware!

As Mordred, frenzied, stretched his hand
To seek Guinevra through the land,
There came a herald, pale with fear,
To tell that Arthur's hosts drew near.
He ordered fire, and Camalot blazed,
Till all its crumbling walls were razed.
He called his warriors, and they go
By roads and passes deep with snow,
A threatening battle-front to bring
Against his uncle and his king.

The shades of night begin to frown
Upon the plains of Barrendown;—

Pine forests these waste plains enclose,
A mighty torrent through them flows;—
Here either army spends the night
In preparation for the fight.

But sleep and slumber come not near
Hearts tortured by hate, doubt and fear;
For not a warrior of them knows
With whom at morning he may close;
Then friend shall pierce the heart of friend—
A brother's life a brother end—
A father smite with murderous knife
The son to whom himself gave life.

Upon his couch grim Mordred lay,
All harnessed, wishing for the day.
Though piercing cold the winter-air,
'T was far too sultry for him there,
As visions of his life appeared,
And images that fancy reared.
He laughed aloud: 'And can it be
That some good spirit weeps for me?

I—I who wear a golden crown,
Here, like some beggar, lay me down;
I fight for what was ne'er my own,—
Before I had possessed it, flown—
What mockery! How can thought divine
A folly infinite as mine?
The labours of my life undone—
My honour, my salvation gone.
But for all deeds I may have done
I am responsible to none!
Then come what may—I'll labour still
My schemes, my ventures to fulfil!'

   But on his cold, uncovered bed,
Arthur his prayer of evening said,
And by the camp-fire sank to sleep;
And through his slumbers, calm and deep,
Rose visions of achievements done,
Of love and battle bravely won.
Then suddenly he seemed to stand,
Alone, at dawning, on the strand;

His wounded head, and half-dimmed sight,
Gave token of a hard-fought fight.
He drew his bugle, but no sound
Broke the unearthly stillness round.
Then he perceived a barge, that bore
Its wondrous burden to the shore;
Like a proud swan it rode along,
Upon its deck a beauteous throng.
Before the masts, with foliage twined,
The sails shine golden in the wind:
He hears a sound of hands that grasp,
Of lips that meet, of arms that clasp:
He sees wide-streaming glories shed
Their halo round Morgana's head.
Mid songs of joy from every lip,
She gently draws him to the ship;
And so they sail, from that lone strand,
To Avalon, to the Holy Land.

IX.

In Scandinavian lore 't is said,
That, when Earth's latest night hath fled,
Upon the expiring world shall rise
The awful dawn of sunless skies,
Life feel its latest throes begin,
Exultant Death its victory win.
Foul crimes shall in that world be done—
The father felled by hand of son;
Kith shall forget the ties of kin,
And fratricidal war begin.
Then earth and world in storm to end,
The Fimbul winter shall descend,
And hail and arrows fall abroad
On that dread day of axe and sword.
Then from the trembling lap of earth
Shall hell's imprisoned folk go forth

To meet, in latest, fiercest fight,
Walhalla's warriors bold and bright.
Not proud with hope, but fierce with rage,
Their grim mute contest these shall wage;
Then Time shall cease, and on that day
In flame the Heavens shall melt away.

 Just such a day began to frown
Upon the woods of Barrendown.

 The snow cleared off, the fog slow rose,
As nearer drew the serried foes;
And front to front, and man to man,
His foeman's features each could scan.
All sound is hushed—then on the ear
Bursts the loud shock of clashing spear,
And many a warrior on the field
Falls heavy, with his cloven shield
The wounded chargers snort and rear,
Mad with excitement, pain and fear;
Hanging in stirrup or to rein,
Half-lifeless corses scour the plain.

Through the deep ranks of warriors there
Rode Arthur: his long silver hair
On purple fell and mail of gold;—
Fixed was his glance, serenely bold,
And mightily aloft he bore
His ancient sword Excalibor.
Sir Lucan rode upon his right,
The cellarer he—a trusty knight;
Upon his left rode Bedivere,
Who bore his wine cup many a year.
About the king they ride,
These twain, on either side,
And through the thickest of the fray
For their imperial lord break way:
Hands that the goblet held aright,
Could hold a manful sword in fight;
And richly as the wine had glowed,
The foeman's purple blood now flowed.

But through the wood of spear and lance,
With eyes that wildly glare and glance,

Breaks Mordred, like some phantom form,
His armour black as night of storm.
On raven steed he spurred along,
Trappings and selle with silver hung;
Red streamed the mantle that he wore,
His shield a flaming dragon bore.
As, breathing slaughters out, he rode,
Death grimly in his footsteps trode,
And soon the latest sun had set
On him who that dread visage met.
Dark were the depths of Mordred's soul
With hate that nothing could console;
He hated fiercely his own heart,
He felt its ceaseless, goading smart;
He only envied those who fell
Beneath his blows—they rested well.

Day waned; but on that battle-field
Still rang the shock of axe and shield.
But fiercest raged the contest round
The close of barricaded ground,

Where the brave monks of Inglewood,
In solemn sable vesture, stood.
In cowl and iron helm they came,
To strike a blow for Mordred's claim;
Saint Hubert's image high they bore,
And by his sacred name they swore.
With his huge club, in wrathful mood,
In front the pious Abbot stood;
He cursed the banded hosts of Korah,
And chaunted, in clear voice, the 'Hora';
The pious brethren concert made,
And bravely fought and bravely prayed.

From the grey East advanced the Night,
But louder, angrier grew the fight.
Then the red blood began to flow
In rivers, through the fields of snow;
The living moved with stumbling tread
Among the bodies of the dead.
'Twilight's last rays began to yield,
As Mordred shouted through the field —

'Ho! fire the wood—we need some light—
There's work enough to do this night!'
His words like flames of lightning fell,
And wrought their work of ruin well.
At once from all the forest broke
Sharp tongues of fire, great clouds of smoke,
And redly through the darkness shone
The glare of flaming pitch and cone.

Then madly through the forest tore,
Scared from his haunt, the forest boar;
The wild ox bellow'd out his fear;
With antlers laid back low, the deer
Leapt, shrieking, over heaps of slain,
And broke through ranks of fighting men.
Singed from the fire, upon their track,
Came wolves and wolves, a grimly pack;
But now no longer lusted they
To spring upon their easy prey—
Unharmed across their path can go
The tender hind, and hart, and roe.

But in that awful hour began
A deadlier strife 'twixt Man and Man;
It seemed more firm the foeman stood,
With feet and ankles in red blood.
Red was the heaven overhead,
The ground beneath their feet was red;
And, but for shield that clashed on shield,
But for the greeting broadswords pealed,
'T would seem that phantoms of the air
And ghostly forms were meeting there.

Sir Markulph was a puissant knight,
He led the lancers to the fight.
From Friesland's distant downs he came,
A Hun of vast and grimly frame.
The giant steed on which he sate
Could scarce support his manly weight.
Across the seas he joined the horde,
With Mordred, of some Viking lord;
And side by side with Mordred he
Had fought by land and fought by sea.

Like a grim bear he fought to-day,
And heaps of dead around him lay.
If not so swift was now his hand,
Yet nothing could its blow withstand.
Loud was the clash, as with his force,
He charged the lines of Arthur's horse:
Their banner fell, their ranks were riven,
And on the frozen torrent driven:
The swollen river angrier flowed,
As on the ice they tramped and trode.
But soon Sir Markulph's work was done:
Struck by a bolt, the mighty Hun
Fell, and his body, with a roar,
Rove all the ice from shore to shore,
And the freed torrent swifter ran
With friend and foe, with horse and man.
Yet clinging to the slippery edge
Of some great floating block or ledge,
With fist and dagger still they wage
Grim contest, in despair and rage,

Until beneath the fatal brink,
Exhausted, one by one they sink,
And choke the huge gorge of the stream
With corpse and mutilated limb.

  Upon a mossy Druid stone
Sat Arthur, weary and alone;
And wistfully his anxious eyes
Gaze through the depths of darkened skies.
Beyond, the woods were burning still,
And clouds of smoke rolled up the hill;
All round the plain beneath he sees
The trunks of burnt and blasted trees,
Whose branches still are glowing hot
With smouldering fire in knur and knot.
A storm of snowflakes falls apace
Upon his sorrow-laden face,
Whereon the eye can trace the pains
That hold his beating heart in chains.
Now all is still—save now and then
The wind some murmur brings again;

From the far distance scarce is heard
The echo of the brandished sword;
But these die out—and not a sound
Breaks on the deathly silence round.
The monarch hearkens, but his ear
The rushing stream alone can hear.
His hands sank slowly by his side,
'Methinks 't is over now,' he cried.

Mute sat the monarch there until
Once more the sun rose on the hill,
And, buried in their graves of snow,
Saw Britain's bravest, best laid low.
There, friends and foemen side by side,
Lay England's glory, Arthur's pride.
But on that field the eye marked one
Who, like a shadow, stalked alone,—
As through a cornfield moveth slow,
A reaper when the sun is low,—
Red-gauntleted and grim, who saith?
Is this King Mordred, or King Death?

Fell from the monarch's head, and rang
His helm, as fiercely he upsprang:
He cried, 'Our work we must not shun,
One thing remains that must be done!'
He raised his spear, the grey old man,
And stoutly upon Mordred ran;
Beneath his helmet's chain he smote
Him sorely, close beside the throat;
Into his shoulder pass'd so well
The spear, that Mordred almost fell.
But when that grimly warrior felt
The wound, he swung his axe, and dealt
On Arthur's unprotected head
A blow so stern, that, hot and red,
Down his white locks the blood was shed.
Then Mordred on that fatal field
Fell, covered wholly by his shield.

'Sir Lucan,' Arthur said, 'thy hand!
And lead me to the Ocean's strand!'—
'Nay,' said Sir Lucan, 'for you lack
All strength; but I upon my back

Will bear you gladly.' Then he bore
The monarch down toward the shore;
But, bleeding from an unseen wound,
Himself fell dead upon the ground.

  Then good Sir Bedvere raised and bore
The monarch to the Ocean's shore.
There sat the king and hearkened long:—
' Hear'st thou the notes of woman's song?
Sir Bedvere now bow down thine ear!
Mine ancient sword, my good sword here,
Take thou to yonder crag, and throw
Far out into the waves below.'
But when Sir Bedvere took the blade,
And saw its haft with gems inlaid,
That richly sparkled, played, and shone,
He laid it lightly on a stone.
' It surely were more harm than good
To sink this sword in yonder flood.'

  ' What word, what word,' exclaimed the King,
' Of my good sword, hast thou to bring?'

'I cast away your ancient sword,
But nothing marked I, good my lord.'
' Sir Bedvere, I have held thee dear,
For thou wert true for many a year;
Now, in this hour when I must die,
Canst look upon my face, and lie?'
Then good Sir Bedvere wept to view
His monarch's face ; so went and threw—
Yet deeply grieving to obey—
Into the waves the sword away.
'What word, what word,' exclaimed the king,
'Of my good sword hast thou to bring?
Hast done, Sir Bedvere, my behest?
The fight is out—I go to rest.'
' In mist and vapour,' he replied,
' A white arm rose above the tide,
Grasped, brandished thrice, and then withdrew
Beneath the waves the sword I threw.'
' Thanks, thanks, Sir Knight: my sacred sword
Is to that spirit-hand restored,

Which gave me, in youth's glorious hour,
That token of my kingly power.
Beneath the waves that beat this shore,
For ever rest, Excalibor!
But sweet, soft music calls away
My spirit, and I would not stay.
I see white-plumaged swans appear,
I see a little barge heave near,
About whose shining mast the vine
And creeper, leaf and tendril, twine.
I see its glorious sails of gold,
See veils that queenly forms enfold!
Morgana, amongst these, I see:
Sweet sister, now I come to thee.
Now all my woes, my griefs are done,
I knew this hour thou wouldst not shun.
Raise me a little, that I lie
Safe on the barge, before I die.—
Bedvere, farewell! for I pass on
To the Holy Land—to Avalon!'

Thus, after his long battle-day,
Earth's greatest, mightiest pass'd away;
And realms of light and glory found
Where Hate and Love no more shall wound.
But ask the Breton, in his land,
Or those who dwell on Cornwall's strand,
To tell how Arthur pass'd away:
In old tradition, these will say,
That Arthur shall return again,
As hero, conqueror, king to reign.
Then land and people shall be free
From the oppressor's tyranny,
And Arthur on that day shall found
A new, a holier Table Round.

Such is the story: eagles soar
Above the rocks on Cornwall's shore;
In Breton woods the nightingale
For ever tells its lovesick tale.

X.

Across the water glode three sail
Flashing with shield, and spear, and mail:
It was Sir Lancelot and his crew,
For he had raised his banner blue,
Which to his feudal lord once more
Its token of allegiance bore.
The anchors settled in the sand,
The eager warriors leapt on land.
On mountain and on glen there lay
The damp fog's misty, leaden grey.
Unwonted gloomed Sir Lancelot's face:
' How fearful is this day, this place!'
He climbed a rocky piece of ground,
And spied out all the land around;
There, in the valley of the fray,
Unnumbered warriors' bodies lay;

And long he sought among the slain
Some trace of life, but all in vain.
Then sadly to his men he came,
And horror shuddered through his frame:
'Pray that in peace may sleep the brave!
Too late, my men, too late to save.'

But as in silence that array
Round the crag's corner wound their way,
There sat Sir Bedvere motionless,
The monarch's head upon his breast.
Half-frozen sat the old man there,
With ice and snow on beard and hair;
But still with joy that soldier brave
A cheer of hail and welcome gave,
And still his voice had power to tell
How all was lost, how Arthur fell.
Then with weak voice and glazing eye,
He grasped the good sword at his thigh:
'Take ye the body of your lord:
I kept true watch and loyal ward.'

Then, without sound or trace of woe,
His dying head sank in the snow.

 The warriors' eyes were wetly dewed,
Silent and pale Sir Lancelot stood:
Shame smote that noble heart of his
To see such loyalty as this.
Then from his men aside he turned,
And glowing thoughts within him burned.
And still he saw before him loom
The Phantom of his cursed doom,
That had passed over in the night,
And reaped Death's harvest in its flight.

 'Forget, O God, the wretch's name
Who sowed the first seeds of this shame!
Woe! never love from grief was free!
And all the joy that glowed through me
Became, in that destroyer's hand,
A wasting and consuming brand.
But now the mighty all are dead
Who linked our bonds of love with dread;

No more pursuit and slavery—
My Guinevere, we both are free.
Ah! endless, endless rolls between
Us two that stream of blood, my Queen!
The joys we did anticipate—
The love—all, all is closed by fate:
Our love must learn, resigned to go
Beneath Heaven's curse—renounce—forego!'

  So spake Sir Lancelot, and peace came
Through all his soul's great grief and shame.
Slow towards his men his steps he bends—
He finds them weeping o'er lost friends.
'Brave young Sir Lyonel, and you
In hour of battle proven true,
Now all is over; but receive
The last command that I shall give.
Here, underneath this great white stone,
Let royal Arthur rest alone!
And let a tomb of granite tower
Above him, where these waters roar,

That passing mariners may gaze
For ever on it in amaze.
And dig you graves, and lay the rest,
A friend and foeman breast to breast.
Then sow this cursèd vale with sand,
That nought may bloom in all the land.
This do, Sir Lyonel, that night
For ever hide our deeds from sight;
Then lead back, with dynastic hand,
My people to their fathers' land.
But I shall wander forth alone.
Farewell! and let none answer, none;
And this I charge you, by the love
Ye bore me, seek not where I rove!'

Loud grieved his faithful men as he
Strode forth alone and silently.
Awhile thro' burn'd and blackened pines
His stately form imperial shines,
Till, lost to their fond gaze, it fades
Away in evening's purple shades.

Then many a weary winter day
They wrought there, while the hours were gray,
And laid at night the dead to rest—
Obedient to their lord's behest.
One hated countenance alone
They found not—Mordred's; then said one—
'Some wolf hath dragged that child of hell
Afar to some dark tarn or dell,
Where, scattered among rocks and stones,
The fog's dank dew shall bleach his bones.'
They raised then, when the rest was done,
A mighty monumental stone,
And went down to the shore to lave
Their hands in ocean's briny wave.
Then sailed off, from that cursèd strand,
Back to their happy fathers' land.

 Through wood and forest Lancelot
Passed, to the vale of Camalot.
Abandoned now lie tower and hall,
And crumbling falls the castle wall.

Close by the margin of the wood,
Beneath a lime, a cottage stood,
In which a sainted man, and old,
His latest days in prayer had told;
But he was dead, and Lancelot gazed,
From that small cottage, down the vale,
Where, in the twilight calm and pale,
Remembered spots the visions raised
Transfigured of his youth again,
With its alternate joy and pain.
Where now are banquet and tournay?
Fight, joy, and love, have passed away.
The pleasures of thy life all seem
The fancies of a vanished dream,
For Beauty's charms and Beauty's wooing
Have been thy curse and thy undoing.

 The vale begins to darkle,
The snowy summits sparkle
In the red light of clouds that lour
About the crumbling castle tower;

And Lancelot stood there, weary, lone,
And wept to think his youth was flown.
Then from the wall he reached him down
The old dead hermit's penance gown,
And laid—but not to rest—his head
Upon the mossy, leaf-strewn bed.
Here the great warrior passed his life,
Far from the world's incessant strife,
And thought how all things here decay,
Till anguish died in calm away.
His will could bid desire depart,
And earnest quiet filled his heart;
But seldom came a stranger-guest
In that lone hermitage to rest;
Though, when the shades of sunset fell,
He ever tolled his evening bell.

The vulture left the battle-ground,
Dark tidings soon were passed around,
Till, through the wild and lonely wood,
They reached Guinevra's solitude.

Then trembled the eye of that lady fair,
And pale she sank and lifeless there.
With death she wrestled twelve long days,
While all things reddened to her gaze:
' In torrents rushing down I see
The blood that ye have shed for me ;
O save me, or these streams of blood
Shall drown me in their purple flood ! '
Her body was to health restored,
But o'er its griefs her spirit poured ;
She saw each dreamy vision swarm
With phantoms of sepulchral form.
No more her smile its glory shed
About her lowly bended head ;
No more she sought with eager lip
Of youth's glad pleasure-cup to sip:
She only sought to weep; but, oh,
The fount of tears refused to flow !

Upon the eve of Christmas-day,
Deep snow on hedge and turret lay ;

And never rang so mournfully
The cloister-bells of Almesbury.
In silent pomp, serene and pale,
To-day Guinevra took the veil.
Her neck of its array was bare;
They cut away her golden hair.
But nought the load of grief shall sever
From that poor heart of hers for ever.
Vain seemed the penance garb she wore,
The cloister's strictest rule and law;
For mass and choral cannot gain
Redemption from the heart's dull pain.
She craved, in ceaseless prayer to God,
The mercies of His chastening rod.

  Men whispered through the orphaned isle
The place of Guinevere's asyle,
And countless pilgrims came to see
The queenly nun of Almesbury.
Meat, drink, and richer gifts she gave,
To every soul that seemed to crave.

One pilgrim, as he left her, said
What life Sir Lancelot now led;
She, bowing, not a word replied—
And, wondering, on his way he hied.

  Time passed, and spring with genial hand
Embraced again the happy land,
And covered with a veil of green
The horrors of the wintry scene.
On the slight twigs that sway and swing,
Once more the finch is chattering;
High o'er the mead, and through the vale,
Are heard the lark and nightingale,
The world's rough ways and works among,
Refraining love's eternal song.
With ivy every rock is bound,
With roses every vale is crowned,
And through yon heaven's blue sky serene
The clouds project their silver sheen.

  Out of the marshland, wrapt in hide,
A man creeps forth with stealthy stride;

Upon his thigh a naked brand,
A clenchèd dagger in his hand;
His beard is long, unkempt his hair,
Black are his eyes and wildly glare,
From their deep hollows flashes bright,
Like madness, oft a quivering light.
In golden sunshine lay the wood
As, breathing heavily, he stood,
And from his lips a whisper came:
'Oh! who shall tell me who I am?
What though they stole my name away,
I must know all on judgment-day.
But foliage shrouds the woods again,
And when shall that day come, oh when?
For ever must I walk alone?
Yes—all the rest are dead and gone!
And yet I know I have one friend,—
If he were found my fears would end.
I call his name to winds and skies,
But no one tells me where he lies:

Mordred! in search of thee I go—
Mordred! thou art not dead, I know.
Mordred! the field with blood was red,
But still I know thou art not dead.
The night was cold, along the ground
Thou crawledst, burning with thy wound;
The wolf and fox were oft thy foe,
Till healed the scar of that stern blow.
I see thee creeping, pale and thin,
The bear's forsaken den within;
Gnawing raw flesh I see thee lie,
Thy banquet-hall heaven's wintry sky.
But run, wretch! stay not freezing here,
Thy shrieks the dead at rest might hear!'

Then, panting through the forest ran,
Up hill and down, the fearful man.
He paused not till, at noon of day,
A deep, still vale before him lay.
In the hot sun, he laid him down
To rest, upon the mountain's crown;

And through the valley's shade and sheen
He cast the glance of wistful e'en.
Half-hid in verdant hedge and wood,
Below the hill a cloister stood;
A narrow pathway, trodden red,
Toward its garden-wicket led :
' I thought in childhood fame to gain
By strife and labour, toil and pain,
And in some peaceful cloister then
To die, at peace with God and men.
Where is the woman that deluded
My soul, and then my grasp eluded?
Fool! she escaped me in the hour
When she was prisoner in my power.
She robbed me of my heaven; but fleet
To follow her shall be my feet.
My parchèd throat is all aglow—
To quench my thirst her blood must flow!'

 A traveller passing down the glade
Before the cloister's wicket staid;

He knocked, and to the threshold came
She who was once King Arthur's dame;
Then that wild wanderer in the wood
Rushed down the hill in grimly mood.

  The traveller passed, and, as he went,
Sang in his heart's full joyousment;
Guinevra, dreaming, stands and sees
Him disappear among the trees:
'God speed, young traveller, thy way—
For thee the world is glad and gay.'
She heard a voice, her startled eyes
Saw suddenly a hand arise:
'Love, art thou mourning still for me?
Sure, none but kings can sue for thee.
Thou livest still, forsaken bride?
The powers of hell are on my side!'
By agony of fear opprest,
She reeled—a dagger pierced her breast.
She turned in terror of surprise
The glance of her death-laden eyes:

'Mordred!' so fell, and pressing tight
Her hands, closed out the horrid sight.

He crushed his hands against his brow—
That sweet voice smote him like a blow;
The chains so long his spirit bound
Were snapped asunder at the sound.
'Mordred! Am I? It is the tone
Of the cherub that sits at the foot of the throne.
What heavenly breezes round me wave,—
How hot my sleep was in the grave!'
He looked around him, and for awe
Stood silent, at the things he saw:
The last illusion left his brain—
He lives, he lives indeed again:
On the red ground before him sleeps
Fair Guinevere, with pale, cold lips.
As often, on a sultry day,
One flash the vapour clears away,
And through the clouds heaven's glad blue light
Breaks forth at once, serene and bright,

So, by love's lightning riven, roll
Away the clouds from Mordred's soul.
But, at the light which on them broke,
Grief, anguish, shame, once more awoke.
His dagger is all red;
He himself hath laid her dead.
And but once more he dared to trace
The features of that glorious face,—
Gazed, as the damned, in their despair,
On realms with light and glory fair:
Then sprang, not daring there to stay,
With restless, tortured thoughts away.

  He wandered, until overhead
The stars appeared, and, purple-red,
The gloaming's heavy clouds were spread—
The hour of slumber, hour of peace,
When weary toil and labour cease.
Then from a chapel, sweet and clear,
A vesper bell broke on his ear,
Which, in that lonely forest there,
The nightly wanderer called to prayer.

Then Mordred paused—but not to pray;
The paths he walks lead far away
From those that guide the sinner's feet
Towards the heavenly Mercy-seat.
But now these chimes before him bring
The days of youth's forgotten spring,
And on his darkened soul there loom
Some tokens of no distant doom.
In his lone heart a longing grew,
A human countenance to view:
It made him well-nigh glad to see
A hermit 'neath the linden tree.

 Mordred approached :—' No need to fear,
Though wild my lineaments appear.
I am a faded, blasted leaf,
Blown from Life's tree by storms of grief;
But grief, repentance, tears are vain—
I come not to you to complain;
I do not ask you to console
Or promise mercy to my soul;

But let me to a Man confess
The sins that vex me and distress.
Thou sinless, holy man, give ear,
I pray you, by God's love, and hear!'
   Without a word the hermit rose,
And drew his habit's cowl more close.
'Of treason hear, thou holy man,
Adultery, murder!' he began.
'In earth's remotest parts my name
Was heralded with pomp and fame.
My Monarch loved me and believed—
My King, whom basely I deceived.
Think! this foul heart of mine could dare
Bring shame upon his hoary hair.
I robbed him of his life and throne—
Can Lucifer with God atone?'
The hermit's cheeks flushed red;
With hollow voice he said,
'God's mercy is for sinful men!'
'Amen,' the wanderer cried, 'Amen.'

'I lived a lone, a steadfast life,
In toil and prayer, in war and strife.
But I too felt the power of sin,
And sought another's spouse to win;
Then for my love, I loved so well,
A great and mighty people fell.'

The hermit's cheeks flushed red;
With hollow voice he said :
'God's mercy is for sinful men !'
'Amen,' the wanderer cried, 'Amen !'

'My heart love never yet had known;
I loved her in the world alone,—
This day, by frantic rage distrest,
I plunged my dagger in her breast!'

The hermit heard, with seething ear,
With flaming eye, a form to fear.
'Guinevra !' but grief crushed and smote
The accents of his faltering throat.
'Mordred, thy deeds may God forgive !
My hands refuse to let thee live !'

He doffed his cowl, his sword he brought,
And in the gay, blue garment, wrought
And woven by Guinevra's hand,
Before that other took his stand.
It was the prize he bore away,
At Camalot, on the tournay-day.

Then suddenly the clouds were riven,
And the full moon shone down from heaven;
But grimly, Mordred, maddening, laid
Both hands upon his naked blade:
'That tale was jest and mockery!
I knew my mortal enemy!'

Unhelmed, unharnessed, thus they stand,—
A naked sword in naked hand.
Brief space they breathe, then grim the fight
Begins, in loneliness and night.
Their brandished swords in circles swept—
They hewed, they foined, they rushed, they leapt;
They traced and traversed, stooped and stood,
Not covert of their might and blood;

And neither heeded that he bled,
Though all the grass with blood was red.
With flaming eyes, with veins aglow,
They fought until their strength sank low;
And fainter now their swords they clasped,
They paled, they paused, for breath they gasped.
From Mordred's lips escaped a cry—
He reeled, he bowed, he fell—to die.

But Lancelot felt his course was run,
And hate and hope for him were done.
Then through the wood, at fullest speed,
A cloisterer came on foaming steed:
'Great lord, the Queen's command I bear—
The grasp of Death lies hard on her:
An unknown hand the dagger bore
That smote her at the cloister-door.
To you, my lord, she bade me fly,
For she would see you ere she die.'
'Dismount,' cried Lancelot; and he leapt
To horse, and through the forest swept.

And as he rode, the pale moon beamed
On the red blood that down him streamed.
He prest his hand upon his side,
To stay life's quickly-ebbing tide;
And, without breathing-space or rest,
His horse he hardly spurred and prest.

Death's hand upon Guinevra lay,
Her lips' sweet red had paled away;
But on her countenance the light
Of peace was shed, serenely bright.
She feels Heaven's mercy dawn again,
Forgiving sin and quenching pain.
She sees, not now with worldly eyes,
The love of other days arise,
Transfigured, sinless, pure and free,
Herald of Immortality.

Serene she lay; he did not enter
And Hope withdrew its peradventure.
She whispered low, 'I thank thee, Heaven!
I feel, I know our sin forgiven.

Far lovelier is it I should not
Behold again my Lancelot,
Until I view, with holier eyes,
To meet me there, his spirit rise.'

  A horse's tramping footsteps fall—
A voice rings through the cloister hall.
Late comes the strange and ghastly lover,
His heart had whispered all was over.
Soft stepped he to Guinevra's bed,
And bowed him down beside her head.
He loosed the hand that prest his heart,
And let the stream of life-blood start;
Upon her head his hand he laid,
And with its golden tresses played;
He smiled, he kissed her;—then beside
Fair Guinevere Sir Lancelot died.

  In consecrated union rest
Those pallid sleepers, breast to breast,
And peace to their cold cheeks imparts
Its glory—peace is in their hearts.

Peaceful and still is that chambère,
But outside, in the morning air,
To spring's delights the garden wakes,
The creeper at the window shakes,
And in the thicket, glad and green,
A birdie hymns the morning in.

ROLAND AND BLANCHEFLEUR.

(A FRAGMENT.)

> Waz aber min lesen do wære
> Von disem sene mære,
> Daz leg ich miner wille kür,
> Allen edeln herzen für.
>
> *Gottfrid of Strasburg,* v. 67.

LOVE is a wondrous thing; love reconciles all contradictions,

Perfecting joy through sorrow, made perfect only through sorrow.

Rising in hope through the purple dawn of youth's beauty and vigour;

Love, at the sunset of life, still points to the land of the Morning.

Love is the ark of safety which saves in the Deluge of Passion.

Love is the bread of the heart; God's manna made
 sweeter through sorrow;
Sweet after sorrow and anguish, as bread is sweet
 after labour.
At the warm welcoming fire, the cheerful glow which
 love kindleth,
Charity warms her cold knees, and drives the chill
 frost from her fingers.
 Ye who would hear a tale of love made perfect
 through sorrow,—
Ye who would know how lovers drink joy from the
 cup of affliction,—
Hear how Roland loved Blanchefleur, how Blanche-
 fleur lived wholly for Roland.
Tales of true love are good for the heart—they feed
 it and warm it,
Rendering mystic, initiate, perfect the heart of the
 hearer.
Come, sweet lovers, and hearken, and learn of Roland
 and Blanchefleur!

Hear how they loved in life, and in death they were
 not divided :
Whispering one to the other, 'I love thee as Roland
 loved Blanchefleur!'
Answering one to the other, 'I love thee as Blanche-
 fleur loved Roland!'
Many kings were of old in Britain, who, living in
 discord,
Preyed on each other's lands and waged continual
 warfare;
Plundering cities and towns, laying waste God's
 bountiful harvest;
Slaying each other's subjects, and taking captive their
 maidens;
So that the land was cursed, and the wealth of the
 island was squandered.
Till, perceiving at length that no good could come of
 their fighting,
All these kings consented together and chose them a
 ruler,

Who should be king of all kings and chief of all chieftains in Britain.

Then they appointed March, who was heir to the earldom of Cornwall,—

March, who ruled his warriors in love and his people in justice,—

Known among men for his truth, for his hatred of wrong and of falsehood,

Brave as the giants of old, yet full of mild love, like a mother.

Then said March: 'By heaven, the land has been cursed through your discords;

Let there be no more fighting, but live in friendship, like brothers.

Hate is the shadow that chills, and love is the sunshine that warmeth!'

March appointed each year a feast, and sent invitation

Through all lands of his realm, to the uttermost parts of the island,

Calling his kings and princes, his earls and barons
together,
Sending welcome to all who would come, with their
wives and their maidens.
May was the month he appointed, and four weeks
lasted the hightime.
May is the fairest month in Britain, the home of the
happy;
May is the daughter of Winter, the mother of Summer
and Harvest;
May is the bride of the Sun, and Love is their off-
spring and Gladness;
Then the trees break forth into bud, and the rose
into blossom;
Then the heart breaks forth into love, and the soul
into gladness,
Love in the heart of the man, and joy in the soul
of the maiden.
May is a gracious queen, that lavishes wealth on her
subjects,

Feeding the eye with beauty, and filling the ear with
enchantment;
Laughing with tears of joy in the dew of the morning
and evening;
Ever, by night and by day, are heard her ministering
angels
Hymning her glory—the lark and the nightingale,
sweetest of singers.

 Every month of May, King March, in Tintagol
Castle,
Welcomed his kings and princes, his earls, his barons,
and nobles;
Kings of fruitful counties, and lords of islands and
marshes;
Knights renowned in battle, right comely in aspect
and bearing;
Men of sinew and muscle, like knotted oaks of the
headland,
Standing firm as the sturdy oaks in the storm of the
battle,

Yet now in milder mood, reflecting the gentleness
 round them,
Spread by their stately dames, and the beauty and
 youth of their daughters,
Even as bud and blossom make lovely the trees of the
 forest.
 Many a feast had been held in Tintagol, many
 a hightime;
Many a knight had brought to his maiden the prize
 of the fairest,
Many a maiden had crowned her knight with the
 prize of the bravest;
Yet was never a knight had earned in the joust and
 the tournay
Half so fairly as Roland the Breton the prize of
 the bravest;
Never a maiden deserved so truly as Blanchefleur,
 the peerless,
Sister of March, the courtly king, the prize of the
 fairest.

Into all lands had reached the fame of Tintagol
Castle,
Over the blowing seas the ships and the breezes had
borne it,
Until it came to Bretagne, to Canoul, on the shore of
the ocean,
Where was the castle of Roland, the youthful king
of the country.
Long had his land lain low beneath the hand of the
stranger,
Who had oppressed the people, and eaten the fruit
of their labour,
Until Roland arose, like the sun that destroyeth
the darkness,
Freeing his land from the foe, and his folk from the
fear of the spoiler;
So that his people had rest, and reaped the fruit of
their harvests.
Never was born of woman a man so perfect in all
things

That make seemly a man, as Roland: so royal in
lineage,
And so kingly in person, so fairly and comely pro-
portioned;
Courteous was he to all, and tender to women and
maidens;
Courteous even to his foes; yet apt to be lightly
offended,
Raging then like a storm on the waves of the boisterous
ocean;
But when the tempest was over, as mild as the sea
which in spring time
Smiles with its thousand dimples, its wavelets of green
and of purple.
Roland heard in his land, in Canoul, on the shore of
the ocean,
How each month of May, King March assembled
about him
All the nobles of England, to pastime, and jousting,
and tournay;

So that his court, with its chivalrous knights and its
  beautiful maidens,
Seemed like a garden laid out by the skilful hand of
  the gardener,
Where were trees to give shade, and flowers to give
  beauty and fragrance.
But, above all, he heard how the kings and nobles of
  Britain,
Tired at length of their wars, of continual discord
  and fighting,
Chose King March to be lord over all the sovereigns
  of Britain;
Seeing they held him to be God's greatest, his bravest
  and wisest,
True to his word himself, and hating falsehood in
  others,
Hating injustice and wrong, and ruling by love and
  by justice.
Then he thought in his heart, and said, 'By heaven,
  't were well now,

I should go to King March and his court in Tintagol
   Castle;
There I shall learn of him to be more courteous and
   gentle,
Truer to God and to man, more knightly to dame
   and to maiden.'
  Then he entrusted the care of his lands to Rual the
     Faithful,—
· Rual li Foitenant was he called in the speech of his
    country,—
Bidding him rule in justice, and root out injustice
   and falsehood,
Succour the weak and oppressed, and welcome kindly
   the stranger.
This he bade him do, and Rual gladly consented,
Ruling the land in justice so long as Roland was absent;
Mightily guarding the land that none should enter
   to spoil it,
Keeping his master's treasures, his castles, his towns,
   and his people.

Meanwhile Roland bade twelve of his knights prepare for the journey,

And with these he sailed from Canoul on the shore of the Ocean.

Certain were all that gazed on the vessel leaving the harbour,

This was the bravest crew, the goodliest ship that had ever

Smiled on the sullen face of dull, monotonous Ocean.

All that was seen of the ship, above the edge of the water,

Gleamed like a rainbow; the planks were of gold and silver and purple;

Broad as the face of a man were the planks, and the purple enamelled,

Laid on a costly metal by cunning device of the workmen.

On the bow of the vessel a dove, in token of friendship,

Shone with its breast of divers colours and pinions of silver;

Also its beak was of silver, and bore a branch of the
olive,
Tokening a message of peace; and a shield was seen
on the vessel,
Having its point turned upward : the costly sails
were of purple,
Curiously wrought with gold, and the flags were of
silk and of satin.
Thus they sailed from Canoul, and the favouring
wind was behind them,
So that they clave a furrow across the fields of the
Ocean,
Straight as the skilful ploughman that tilleth the
land with his oxen.
And on the seventh day the turrets of Tintagol
Castle
Gladdened their hearts in the golden gleam of the sun
at its dawning.
Then they made for the beach, and Roland, glad of
his beauty,

Proud of his manly vigour, arrayed himself in his brightest.
First he drew on his vest and his doublet of costliest linen,
Wrought and embroidered with gold by his damsels; both were of scarlet:
Over these a surcoat of damask bordered with jewels,
Gleaming like the broad fringe that lights the horizon at dawning;
On his feet were low shoes of curious Corduan leather,
Clasped with bosses of gold, devised in the form of a lion.
Only his legs were bare, and all that saw were astonished
At the bold sinews of iron, th' heroic strength of the muscles.
Over his shoulder and under his arm, a cloth of blue-purple

Bore four apples of gold, each fourscore cattle in value.

Further a cross of red gold, of the hue of the lightning of heaven,

Hilted the sword at his thigh, its temper blue-green like the ocean.

Lastly, he threw over all a mantle of flame-coloured satin,

And round his curling hair he clasped a circle of rubies.

Also he bade his knights array themselves, each in his noblest,

To do honour to March and to him. Then they anchored their vessel,

And descending in boats, they rode towards Tintagol Castle.

On the greensward that lay round the castle, King March and his nobles,

With their dames and their maidens, were sunning themselves in the pleasant

Morning of May, and hearkening the song of the birds
in the branches.

Tents of cloth of damask and satin studded the
meadows,

And before these the guests reclined on cushions of
velvet;

Knights and ma'dens were resting beneath the sweet
shade of the lindens,

Talking of dance and of tourney, and wit and beauty
were sparkling,—

Wit from the lips of the knights, bright smiles from
the eyes of the maidens.

Then was word brought to King March, that a
vessel lay in the haven,

Bearing tokens of peace, the dove and the shield with
point upward.

And the messenger said, 'Lord! never in Tintagol
Castle

Saw I such splendid guests as are coming in boats
from the vessel.'

Then rejoiced in his heart the gentle king, and descending
Toward the low beach, he awaited, and courteously welcomed the strangers.
Roland gladly told King March the cause of his coming,
Saying, 'Lord, I would learn of you to be knightly and courtly,
True before God and man, and gentle to lady and maiden:
For I have heard that all men in Britain, the home of the happy,
Hold you to be God's greatest and best, His bravest and wisest.'
Courtly March replied, 'To be God's greatest and wisest
Who should lay claim? *I* surely least and latest of all men,—
I who entertain here so many greater and wiser,
Braver and better than I am, I only count myself happy

That they honour me here by their presence; we learn
from each other,
And I doubt not, if you will bide with us here, it
shall happen
That we all learn from each other to be both greater
and wiser.'
So were their hearts made glad by the courteous
greeting and welcome.
When they went to the palace, King March called
Blanchefleur his sister,
Bidding her serve his guest with water, for so was
the custom.
Then she gladly consented, and brought a basin of
silver,
And an ivory jug with water, and cloths of fine
linen,
And would herself have washed his face, but he
would not her service,
Yet, that he might not wound her, refusing gently and
knightly.

Then they passed to the hall to partake of the generous
    banquet:
Meet had been both banquet and hall for the Em-
    peror Arthur;
Meet for the knights of the Table Round the chairs
    and the couches,
Covered with scarlet and fur, and framed of cedar
    and sandal.
Not a nail could be seen in the hall but was painted
    in gorgeous
Colour, enamelled on gold by cunning device of the
    workmen;
Every pannel around the hall, from the floor to the
    ceiling,
Showing the skill of the painter in subjects taken
    from tourney,
Taken from hunting and hawking, or, what was
    dearer to many,
Picturing tales of true love with its moments of bliss
    and of sorrow.

Red was the wine in the cups, and costly the food in
    the dishes,
Flesh of the boar, and dainty birds, the swan and the
    peacock,
Boar for the stalwart men, and birds for the delicate
    maidens.
  But when Roland had gladdened his heart with wine
    and with feasting,
Lifting his eyes, he gazed around on the dames and
    the maidens,
Clothed in scarlet and purple, in silk and satin and
    sendalle;
Then his eye ever returned to one, to Blanchefleur
    the peerless,
Resting, in glad surprise, on the beauty ingrained in
    her nature.
Tawny with gold, like the flower of the broom, were
    the locks of the maiden,
Falling over her shoulders, that glistened between
    like a river,

Sparkling with silver waves, through the leafy boughs
of the forest;
White as the foam of the wave was her skin, as the
bloom of the crystal;
Fairer her hands than the blossoms of flowers in the
spray of the fountain.
Just as, after the sun has shot the last ray of his
lightning,
Islands of purple float upon silver seas through the
heavens,
So were her eyes; and her cheeks, when the glance of
Roland stayed on her,
Red as the reddest rose that blooms in the Valley of
Wonders.
Softly fell on her cheek the long fringe of her eyelid,
as Roland
Gazed on the delicate face and imperial form of the
maiden;
Then were initiate in love the hearts of Roland and
Blanchefleur.

Let love be the burden
    Of your song, ye mystic!
All things great and good are heard in
    Love's exalted distich.

Hearken thro' this dawning
    Love's Memnonian murmur,
In the golden-purple morning
    Feel your hearts grow warmer.

Mortal youth and maiden—
    Swing love's wondrous censer,
Till all earthly things are laden
    With a perfume denser.

Take love's golden money,
    Buy your hearts meet nurture,
Buy the nectar and the honey
    Of true joy and virtue,

ROLAND AND BLANCHEFLEUR.

Till the glowing passion
  Of your higher nature
Burn the ingrained evil fashion
  Of the lower creature.

*   *   *

That was their marriage-night; and the lone star that
    peered through the window,
Gleamed like a tear of joy on the face of nature above
    them.

ADONIS.

(BION.)

I MOURN for Adonis: Adonis is dead,
    Fair Adonis!
And loud are the Loves in their sorrow: Adonis is
    Fair Adonis!   [dead,
Ah! Venus, no more in thy vesture of purple adorning
    Lie sleeping!
Rise! disconsolate, rise in the dark stole of mourning,
    And, beating
Thy breast, let men hearken thine anguish: Adonis
    Fair Adonis!   [is dead,

I mourn for Adonis, and loud are the Loves
    In the wail of their mourning!
On the mountains Adóne in his beauty is lying,
    The last breath of his breathing—

For a white tusk has pierced his white thigh to the
    Venus sucks wildly weeping.   [dying—
And dark flows the blood down his limbs' snowy
    His eyes in their deadness   [whiteness;
Lie fixed 'neath his brow; from his lips all their
    The rose of their redness,   [brightness,
Is parting, and colder upon them the kiss is
    Venus clings to more bold now;
But he knows not, Adonis—how fondly she presses
    His lips that are cold now!

I mourn for Adonis, and loud are the Loves
    In the wail of their mourning!
Cruel, cruel the wound in the thigh of Adonis;
    But, ah, Cytherea!
More cruel, I ween, and a deeper thine own is,
    In thy heart, Cytherea!
Round that loved one his dogs, faithful ever, are
    The nymphs on the mountain   [moaning;
Weep and wail for Adonis: and Venus is roaming
    Thro' forest, by fountain,

Disconsolate, reft of her comely adorning,
    No shoes on her feet now,
No braid round her hair flowing wildly, she scorning
    All care that is meet now.
And loud in her wail thro' the long ravine speeding,
    All comely—all naked—
The bramble is red with the drops of her bleeding,—
    Big drops that are sacred.
' My Assyrian!' she cries: ah! how anguished her
    ' Sweet, my lord; my Adonis.'   [tone is!
But dark on his breast, once so wondrous in whiteness,
    Like the snow in its sparkling,
From his thigh to his bosom, empurpling their bright-
    The red blood is darkling.   [ness,

Woe, woe, Cytherea! how loud are the Loves
    In the wail of their mourning!
She hath lost her brave lord, and the form of her
    Hath lost its divine.   [beauty
By thy grace and thy beauty, sweet Venus, men
    When Adonis was thine.   [knew thee,

Woe, woe, for thy beauty all died with Adonis!
    The oaks and the mountains
All murmur and echo: ' Woe, woe, for Adonis!'
    The rivers and fountains
All sorrow with Venus, whose woes are at sorest:
    And the flowers deepen redly,
And the dirge of Cythera is heard thro' the forest,
    Thro' the woods ever sadly.

Woe, woe, Cytherea! Adonis is dead,
    Fair Adonis!
And echo made answer: ' Adonis is dead,
    Fair Adonis!'
Ah! who would not have wept o'er so woeful a love
    As Dione's?
When she saw, when she spied the deep wound of
    The red blood flowing darkly   [Adóne,
From his thigh which was withering, then she made
    Her arms reaching starkly—   [moan—
' Stay, Adóne—stay, poor hapless Adóne, till I reach
    The last time for aye!   [thee

Till once more I embrace thee, and fold thee, and kiss
    Lip to lip, as we lie.   [thee
Ah! wake but one moment; once more, ere thy dying,
    Kiss me once more, my own!
As long as there's life in the kiss of thy sighing,
    So long kiss me, Adóne!
Till my mouth suck thy last breath deep into my soul,
    And I drink the dear cup
Of thy charmance, and drain the last drops as they roll,
    Until love be drunk up.
And I'll keep that last kiss, as if it were Adóne
    Himself, fondly and truly.
For thou, my poor lover, poor mourned one, art gone;
    Thou hast left me unduly!
Thou hast gone a long journey, Adonis, to Hades,—
    To the King stern and dread;
And *I* live, nor can follow thee, such my hard fate is,
    To the home of the dead.
Now take him, Persephone,—take him, my husband—
    Thou art greater than I,

And all that is lovely must rest in thy bosom;
    I must fear thee and sigh
For Adóne: he is dead, and I never shall tire
    Out my grief, broken-hearted.
Thou art dead! thrice desirèd, and all my desire
    Like a dream has departed.
And my Cestus is lost with thee: ah! why so wildly
    Intent upon fronting
The beasts of the forest, thou fashioned so childly,
    With the spear of thy hunting?'

Thus did Venus make mourning, and loud are the Loves
    In the wail of their mourning.
Woe, woe, Cytherea! Adonis is dead,
    Fair Adonis!
Venus sheds a big tear for each drop, as it flows,
    Of the blood of Adonis.
From his blood as it falls to the ground springs a rose,
    From her tears anemònies.
I mourn for Adonis: Adonis is dead,
    Fair Adonis!

And loud the lament and the dirge of the Muses,
    But he recks not of these now;
'Tis not that he will not, but Cora refuses
    To give him release now.
Ah! cease, Cytherea, awhile from thy tears and
    Heart-beating;
There shall come a meet time for thy grief, a due
    For weeping!   [season

PET NAMES.

I will call thee all names that are sweet, My Love,
    All names that are fondest and dearest;
That languish on lips as they meet, My Love,
    Breathing murmurs, — Love's language that's clearest.

For the daystar of love hath arisen, Dear Child,
    And dawned on this heart of mine;
And never saw dreamer in vision, Dear Child,
    A ray that was so divine.

And a hope-spring hath welled in my heart, Beloved,
    When my heart was all dry for love;
And that thirsty land is refreshed, Beloved,
    And green as a summer grove.

Wondrous fair is the flower of thy beauty, Sweet,
    And its fragrance is wholly rare;
And the blush of the coyness of duty, Sweet,
    Breathes a bloom ineffable there.

Thy hair is all golden, all golden, Darling,
    Sunbeams play in thy golden hair :
When its tresses are loosely folden, Darling;
    And fall over thy purple chair.

The bloom on the full ripe peach, Ma Belle,
    In the light of the sun's red dying,
Is not so soft as thy cheek, Ma Belle,
    Dewed with just one tear of love's sighing.

And through the bower of thy tresses, Love,
    Glints the whiteness of thy bosom;
Like the sheen of a river which presses, Love,
    Through bowers of fragrant blossom.

Thy lips are like a rich grape, Sweet Heart,
    Ripened in love's atmosphere,
And wines of rich odour escape, Sweet Heart,
    When they're pressed by the touch that is dear.

Thy hands are so soft and so small, My Pet,
    And the veins are so very blue,
In the sunlight so rosy withal, My Pet,
    Those dear hands thrill me through.

And thy feet,—ah! give me thy slipper, Child,
    When this heart of mine is cold,
I will warm it with wine from that beaker, Child,
    Like the Sarmate men of old.

But a costlier drink is mine, Sweet Love,
    And more royal-rare, I ween;
Ay, more royal-rare than the wine, Sweet Love,
    Of Egypt's enamoured Queen.

For jewels that glance like stars move, My Own,
    In those dear, deep eyes of thine;
And those jewels melt into love, My Own,
    And I drink that wondrous wine.

From a goblet more precious, more noble, Dear,
    That wondrous wine I sip,
Than once in the banquet of purple, Dear,
    Trod on haught Belshazzar's lip.

And I'll drink of the draught of thy beauty, Fondest,
    Till the vein of passion fill me!
And raise the rich goblet duly, Fondest,
    Till the merry madness fill me.

Then I'll call thee all names that are sweet, My Love,
    All names that are fondest and dearest,
That languish on lips as they meet, My Love,
    Breathing murmurs — Love's language that's clearest.

LOLA.

A ROMANCE OF INDIA.

By the portals of her palace
  With her cheek upon her hand,
Glinting through the slender trellis
  Of her fingers, laced and spanned
By the waving locks which fall,
Like a dark vine down the wall,
From the frontlet-gem she wears,
Bright as that great Shiva bears,
To the red gold round her waist,
Diamond-studded, jewel-traced,
Lola lies in pensiveness,
For her heart's great loneliness.

She is slender, she is slight
As the pale flower of the night;
Her large eyes are like two seas,
With a purple isle on each,
Where the fireflies play, half-hid
By the shades of either lid.
Soft her lips are pressed together,
Upper lying on the nether,
Like a ripe pomegranate, laid
On a dark grape purple-red.

Truth! when Lola speaks, the word
   Trembles down her radiant lips,
   As the morning dewdrop slips
Down a rosebud to the sward.
And no dreamer in his cave
By the golden-lighted wave,
 Ever fashioned in his aëry
Castle, built by hands of faëry,
Such an oriel set with pearls,
Opening thro' the embowering curls,

When between her lips apart,
Lola warbles out her heart.

Soft and white is Lola's ear,
Starlit by the pearls that peer
Through the dark clouds of her hair.
Oh! its whiteness is more rare,
It is purer than the breast
Of a white swan on its nest,
Where the sparkling water laves
The red lotus with its waves.

On the branches of the trees,
Trembling with the evening breeze,
Birds red-plumaged, yellow-pied,
Silver-pinioned, purple-dyed,
Warbling through their little throats
Unpremeditated notes,
To her fancy seem to say,
'Lola's heart is sad to-day;

She lies restless on her couch,
Caring not her lute to touch;
And she moves not to the hall,
Where her maids hold festival.
Is there poison in the chalice?
Are there serpents in the palace?
Sweetest lady, Lola, say,
Will you languish life away?
There is one who sighs, and waits
All day at the garden-gates;
Think! the flowers of beauty fade,
Sunshine darkens into shade!
Think! the moon of love must wane,
On the dark eye's diaphane!'

On the branches, one by one,
Wakening with the morning sun,
Birds red-plumaged, yellow-pied,
Silver-pinioned, purple-dyed,
Warble thro' their little throats
Unpremeditated notes,

That to Lola seem to say,
' Lola's heart is glad to-day:
There is none who stands and waits
For Lola at the garden-gates;
But a fallen pearl lies there—
Did it drop from Lola's hair?
And a red flower might be found,
Which lies withering on the ground
Can it be the flower which pressed
Yestereven Lola's breast?
It is well it should be so—
Beauty vanishes like snow;
Fairest flowers must soonest fade,
Sunshine darkens into shade;
And the moon of love must wane,
On the dark eye's diaphane!'

EFFIE.

The evening star is setting; ere it get
   Beneath th' horizon, my own vesper star—
The lone-star of my love—my hope—shall set,
   And leave my night of life dark all afar.

For at the setting of that star, my own,
   My loved, too lovely Effie is to be
Another's bride, and I sit here alone,
   To think of all that might have been—and thee!

I call thee mine—my own—another's bride:
   Yes, mine for ever, though, beloved in vain,
Thy trembling heart beats at another's side,
   His all the joy of thee, and mine the pain.

For are not our experiences parts
   Of our own being? Great, true thought divine!
For all the experiences of *our* hearts
   Are mutual: mine are thine, and thine are mine.

And yet I know that, when you read this letter,
   You'll laugh; perhaps think I write but to annoy
And pain you; purse your little lips together,
   And say, ' You foolish—foolish—foolish boy!'

My love! I have been foolish—I am wiser;
   I loved too foolishly, and—and too well;
But deep down in my heart of hearts there lies a
   Word which, though it shall pain you, I must tell.

Better that you should suffer this brief pain—
   Shed o'er these memories one burning tear—
Than that the dropping of continual rain
   Should wear your little heart out, Effie dear!

Therefore I must not spare you. Sharp to sever—
    Keen as the edge of the Archangel's sword,
Shall be the anguish—scorching like a fever—
    Hot as the burning frost-fire of the Lord.

Do you remember—ah! you do—that day
    Beneath the linden-tree, by the broad river,
Whose murmuring waters ne'er again shall play
    Responsive to our hearts' love-tremulous quiver?

And I was jealous of a roguish sunbeam
    That played among your tresses loosely folden,
On your red lips, your snowy breast; and one beam
    Kissed the dear blue of your great eye, all golden.

You had a thornless white rose in your hand—
    I would not trust you with a thorny rose:
I said, 'You must not hurt your little hand;
    There never were such soft, dear hands as those.

You smiled, ' Your hands are not less soft than mine,
    dear !'
And then you slowly pulled the rose-leaves out,
And whispered soft—only a lover's fine ear
    Could hear you, as the breeze strewed them about—

' Un peu—beaucoup—passionnément—pas du tout !'
    The last leaf—' pas du tout;' and so to prove me,
You looked up in my eyes and laughed—' Is't true,
    The naughty rose says that you do not love me ?'

I think I did not tell you that I did;
    But our lips gave a surer, sweeter token;
And so I drew a book out, and we read,—
    Our reading by our quick heart-beating broken:

It was of Abelard and Eloise,
    Their sweet lives, their unutterable bale—
Of Eloisa prostrate on her knees,
    ' The shrines all trembling, and the lamps all pale.'

Now in her breast Faith, Hope serenely rise,
    And waft her spirit to the blest abode,
Now 'with one glance of those deluding eyes,'
    The lover rivals—more than rivals God.

Your lips were trembling—but my heart still sees
    The whisper of your deep-blue eyes divine;
They smiled, 'Sweet lover, we shall rival these,
    For Eloisa knew no love like mine.'

Too dear, too fatal memory of that hour,
    Our hearts had languished into love like death,
Our quivering lips too trembled to have power
    To give our hearts the utterance of breath!

Oh, that was love!—oh, that was no dissembling!
    My sweetest, do I pain you?—it is right—
It must be—think you what hot tears are trembling
    Down my pale cheek, love-blasted, as I write.

Bear with me, therefore, sweetest! I have more
    And far more bitter words to write, and you
Must tremble yet again. There lies before
    My burning eyes a letter, all wet through

With tears I never thought to shed upon it.
    It was wet once before—with tears of joy:
What joy! I think I should not have foregone it,
    Even had I known the sorrow that is now.

You wrote that letter in that curst, dear hour,
    When yet your soul was trembling with the fancies
Which had been waked by the sweet poet's power
    Who wrote of Eloise, and with the glances,

All love-enchanting, of your lover's eyes:
    The poet's frenzy had inspired you, child;
Perhaps his spirit gave you power to rise
    To such a note of love, so wayward-wild.

You wrote you loved me—loved me! In that word
  I felt far wiser, happier than learning
Can make earth's wisest; I knew *all* I cared
  To know. This, child, was your impassioned yearn-
    ing:

' And when that hour, of which we only know
How dread its aspect, and how stern its woe:
When that dark hour approach—and come it must,
Corruption's conquest o'er our failing dust—
When Death above thy darling form, true lover,
Spreads his inevitable wings to hover:
When pales on thy fair cheek the rosy bloom,
Touched by the icy angel of the tomb:
Then, oh! may Heaven grant answer to my prayer,
That in that moment I be near thee there;
That I those locks, dear locks, once more may twine,
As once they mingled in embrace with mine;
And, when its latest sparkle fade, that I
May gently close that once love-rolling eye;

On those pale lips a warmer kiss impress,
Than ever waked thee from thine earthly rest;
May weep one tear that to thy soul shall speak,
In trembling cadence, down thy death-cold cheek;
Clasp thee—how fondly! and without a sigh,
Oh grant me, Heaven!—I ask no more—to die!'

You tremble, sweet! Ah, those were burning words!
   I tremble too, how, you cannot divine;
Your tender frame of woman has no chords
   To bear such high-strained agony as mine.

Oh! if there is a sight could melt to tears
   Perdition's darkest son beneath the sky,
It is not prostrate Eloisa's fears—
   It is the strong man in his agony.

'It is enough!'—no, not enough—not yet.
   I have a sterner thing than these to say:
Think, I can bear it—that lone-star long set.
   Do you remember, on a darker day,

Low on her couch, by nights of anguish worn,
   Your mother lay, life's immortality
Upon her eye, corruption round her form—
   Death's bow wide-strained to let the arrow fly?

Pale her loved cheek: the impress of decay
   Deep in the lineaments of that high brow;
In filial reverence we kiss away
   The trembling tear, and meekly, meekly bow.

That was a dearer whisper than them all;
   You whispered on the hot flush of my cheek,—
'Our Father's will be done! Come, let us fall,
   My *brother*! We can pray,—we cannot speak!'

'Sweet brother!' Sweetest sister!' on our knees
   We prayed in silence by that lone bedside:
A whisper, these her latest accents, these,—
   'Daughter, behold thy husband;—Son, thy bride!'

Now all is over : from my gazing eyes
    The evening star has set : I write no more,
I look out lonely on the starless skies,
    The day behind me and the night before.

But I will walk out bravely in that night,
    Will be a man, will calm these swelling tears,
Stretch forth my arms to holy deeds, and bright
    Shall be *their* starlight, in these gloomy years.

Each deed of this now trembling hand shall glow
    With blessing; trust thou, too, and it may be, love,
Our sorrows were all mercy; I shall know
    When once in Heaven I meet my God—and thee, love!

THE EYES WHICH JESUS LOVED.

> 'Gli occhi da Dio diletti e venerati,
>   Fissi nell' orator ne dimostraro
>   Quanto i devoti prieghi le son grati.'
>
> DANTE, *Paradiso*, xxxiii. 39.

I.

PAINTER, hath thy fancy wandered
  O'er the fairest scenes of Earth?
In long musing hast thou pondered,
  Whence comes Inspiration's birth?
Still aspiring,
Fancy firing
  Every vein that throbs with thought,
  Not too wisely hast thou sought.

II.

Was the Earth, great Earth, too common
  For thy high heroic soul?
In the wide realm of the human,
  Was there no sufficient goal?
In thine aëry
Land of faëry,—
  In the worlds of the Unreal
  Hast thou sought thy fond ideal?

III.

Courage, painter—noble painter,—
  Shadows yet have been thy chase:
Let thy true heart not grow fainter,
  Learn to run a nobler race;
In the Real
Lives the ideal,—
  True art lies concealed in Nature
  In *expression*, not in *feature*.

IV.

Oh! my painter, know thy duty,
   Learn thy high-appointed strife,—
To express the soul of beauty
   In the lineaments of life.
Brave heart, cheer thee !
One is near thee
   In the work thou hast to do,
   Silent prophet of the True.

V.

Not alone in grandest action
   Of the hero's high emprise,
Breathes the heaven-born soul of passion :
   In deep, loving, silent eyes,—
Eyes of woman,
Sweetly human—
   Stillest, brightest passions light
   Depths, like ocean's in the night.

VI.

Oh! had I a skilful right-hand,
　Such high venture to essay,
Woman's love and woman's light, and
　Woman's goodness to portray ;—
Grace of beauty,—
Fire of duty—
　Lovely, intensely fixed, and sure—
　Love immaculately pure ;—

VII.

Not from fabled Grecian islands,
　Not from Paphos' magic shore,
Not from proud Olympus' highlands,
　Not from Venus' sea-foam bower ;
Not from aëry
Land of faëry,
　Where thought wanders, fancy-free,
　Should my inspiration be.

VIII.

Beaming thro' the vista'd ages,
   In the memoried halls of Time
Filled with poets, prophets, sages,
   All of those man calls sublime—
There thou shinest,
Thou divinest,
   Soul of heavenly in the human!
   Soul of angel, form of woman!

IX.

O Madonna—O my lady!
   All my poet-painter's art
I would fain exhaust, to pay thee
   The full tribute of my heart:
Oh, how queenly,
How serenely,
   'Neath those eyelids tear-ymoved,
   Beam those eyes which Jesus loved!

X.

As thy lips kissed infant Jesus,
  From thy loved eyes—oh, so fair!—
Rays of gladness smiled on Jesus,
  Sunbeams kissed His golden hair:
Then more finely,
More divinely,
  Mirrored in His eyes they moved,—
  Those dear eyes which Jesus loved!

XI.

Virgin Mother! even *our* mother
  We may call thee, for we know
Who hath called himself our Brother,
  And we meekly call Him so;
Oh! our Mother,
Not another
  In all time so blest hath proved,
  For thine eyes hath Jesus loved.

XII.

In that mystery of temptation,
  On the mountain's lonely height,
When the angelic high creation
  Gazed upon that wondrous sight—
While His sadness
Wrought our gladness,
  It may be those eyes had power
  To console that awful hour.

XIII.

In that hour when friends forsook Him,
  And a *man's* false kiss betrayed—
When the soul's great anguish shook Him,
  It was *woman's* look that stayed;
When upturning,
Filled with burning
  Tears, those eyes were raised to Jesus,
  Those dear eyes beloved by Jesus!

XIV.

Then, my soul, what inspiration
   Ever fanned so large a fire?
Say, my soul, on what creation
   Of the painter's high desire,
Love and beauty—
Heavenly duty—
   Such divine enchantment moved
   As those eyes which Jesus loved?

GOOD NIGHT.

'Come, my Angel, sweetest Angel,
    Lift thy silvery voice to God:
Hark! the curfew bell is tolling;
    Raise thine infant prayer to God.

'Hark! the fishermen are singing;
    Hymns of evening fill the air;
Jesus listens to their voices;
    Jesus loves our people's prayer.
Look! the waters sparkle, sparkle
    In the moonbeams, as they play,
While above the distant hillside
    Sails her silvery bark away.

'Come, my Angel, sweetest Angel,
   Lift thy silvery voice to God :
Hark ! the curfew bell is tolling ;
   Raise thine infant prayer to God.

'Far beyond these shining waters
   There are other shores that rise,
Glorious shores whence angel-children
   Guide our lov'd ones through the skies.
Where yon golden sun low setteth,
   Lie the islands of the blest :
There hearts, weary with the journey
   Of life's troubled waters, rest.

'Come, my Angel, sweetest Angel,
   Lift thy silvery voice to God.
Hark ! the curfew bell is tolling ;
   Raise thine infant prayer to God.'

Soft she kissed her mother's lips, and,
    Little hand on little heart,
Effie knelt, her God addressing,
    Praying childlike, without art.
But upon the dear child's eyelids
    Sleep fell heavy as she prayed,
In her mother's arms she slumbered,
    Hearing not the voice that said:

' Come, my Angel, sweetest Angel,
    Lift thy silvery voice to God;
Hark! the curfew bell is tolling,
    Raise thine infant prayer to God.'

www.ingramcontent.com/pod-product-compliance
Lightning Source LLC
LaVergne TN
LVHW021112270725
817173LV00009B/702